Collana "I Fornelli"

3

I.W.F.A - International Food & Wine Association
info@ifwa.us www.ifwa.us

Thank you to our sponsor *'Connextions Group Inc'.*
Without their support this book would not have been possible.

Special thanks to all of those who assisted us in gathering together these wonderful recipes. Your help and collaboration is appreciated.

I[a] edizione - maggio 2008
I[a] ristampa - giugno 2009
II[a] edizione aggiornata con nuove ricette - marzo 2011
I[a] ristampa II[a] edizione - luglio 2012

ISBN 88 6039 209 1

# *Good Tastes of Tuscany*©

## Tuscan kitchen recipes

The '*International Food and Wine Association*' aims to bring together lovers and connoisseurs of food and wine and everything it represents. It gives us immense pleasure to share with you, our members and other lovers of Tuscan food this collection of well researched and well sampled authentic recipes.

We invite you to come and try your hand in our Tuscan kitchen and participate in one of our fun and informative cooking classes.
Feel free to peruse our website www.ifwa.us for more information on the cultural courses offered.

# *Antipasti*

## Starters

# *Fettunta*

## Toasted bread with olive oil

Meaning 'oily slice', fettunta can be served as an antipasto or a nibble to be eaten at any time. Simply toast the bread, rub with garlic and then top with salt, freshly ground pepper and a very good extra virgin olive oil.
Fettunta can be also served topped up with 'cavolo nero' (black-leaf kale) or beans, which are also known as cannellini beans.
At the time of the olive harvesting and pressing the fettunta is eaten daily to enjoy the sharp and peppery flavour of Tuscan extra virgin olive oil.
Olives from the Chianti region in particular are known to produce the best olive oil in the world.

# *Bruschetta*

## Tomato and basil toasts

Serves 4

- 2 large ripe tomatoes, diced
- 2 - 3 garlic cloves, peeled
- 8 basil leaves, ripped
- extra virgin olive oil
- salt and pepper
- 300 g Tuscan-style bread

Cut the tomatoes in half, remove the seeds then dice.
Mix the tomatoes, basil leaves, oil, salt and pepper together in a bowl. Set aside for at least 15 minutes. Toast the bread and rub one side with a garlic clove. Spoon the tomato mixture onto the bread and serve. Crostini and bruschetta are always done in the OVEN and NOT under the grill.

# *Crostini di polenta*

## Fried polenta crostini

Serves 4

- 175 g polenta (corn meal)
- ½ L water or stock
- a pinch of salt
- a pinch of black ground pepper

Boil the water or the stock with salt and pepper and slowly pour the polenta into the liquid, whisking continuously. Keep stirring and cook for about 20 minutes. Pour the polenta onto a tray and spread it until you obtain a thickness of about 1 cm. Let it cool. When the polenta is set, cut it into squares and fry these in hot frying oil. Serve with wild mushrooms or chicken liver patè.

# *Crostini ai funghi*

## Mushroom crostini

Serves 6

- 300 g porcini or another kind of wild mushrooms
- 1 garlic clove
- 2 sprigs of catnip or wild mint
- 2 tbs extra virgin olive oil
- a pinch of salt
- a pinch of pepper
- 400 g Tuscan-style bread

Clean the mushrooms with a damp cloth, dice them finely. Lightly sautè the garlic, then add the mushrooms, catnip leaves, salt and pepper. Cook for a few minutes. Slice and toast the bread then place the mushrooms onto each crostino.

# *Crostini ai fegatini*

## Chicken liver crostini

Serves 6

- 350 g chicken livers
- ½ onion sliced
- ½ carrot chopped
- 3 tbs extra virgin olive oil
- 1 tbs capers
- 3 anchovy fillets
- ½ a glass of dry white wine
- vegetable broth or water
- 1 knob of butter
- 500 g Tuscan-type bread

This is also known as 'Crostini Toscani' and is the most traditional topping used in this region. It is similar to a patè.
Sautè the onion and carrot in 3 spoonfuls of olive oil. Add the chicken livers. When they start to brown, add the wine and let it evaporate. Then add a glass of broth or water, the capers and anchovies and let the mixture cook for around 20 minutes. Add the butter and process the mixture in a food processor. Add salt and pepper to taste. Slice and toast the bread then spread the mixture onto each crostino.
Another version of this recipe is to add "Vin Santo" wine which is a typical Tuscan dessert wine instead of the white wine.

# *Crostone al cavolo nero*

## Little toasted bread with black cabbage and sausage

Serves 4

- 500 g black cabbage
- 1 Italian sausage
- 1 onion
- extra virgin olive oil
- salt and pepper to taste
- 50 g grated cheese (parmesan or 'pecorino' which is a hard sheep cheese from Tuscany)
- vegetable broth
- 400 g Tuscan-style bread

Remove all hard parts of the cabbage leaves so you are left with only the leafy parts. Dice the onion and cut up the sausage into small pieces.
Add some extra virgin olive oil to a frypan, then fry the onion, together with the sausage for 5 minutes.
Add the cabbage leaves, then pour over some white wine so that the leaves wither and reduce.
As soon as the wine has evaporated, add a small amount of vegetable broth to stop the cabbage from browning. Take off the heat.

Spoon the cabbage mixture onto toasted pieces of bread, then sprinkle with grated parmesan or pecorino (hard sheep) cheese.
Place in an oven of 180 degrees for 2 minutes to melt the cheese.
For vegetarians this recipe can also made without the sausage.

............................................................

............................................................

............................................................

............................................................

# *Crostini di salsiccia e stracchino*

## Toasted bread with sausage and stracchino cheese

Serves 4

- 1 large loaf of bread or a French Bread stick
- 3 Italian sausages
- 200g stracchino cheese

Cut the skin of the sausage and remove the meat. Mix together the stracchino cheese and the sausage mince. Once mixed well, spread generously onto the bread slices and then place in a pre-heated convention oven for 5 minutes. Serve hot.

# *Crostini con melanzane grigliate e pecorino*

## Eggplant and pecorino cheese crostini

Serves 6-8

- 2 eggplant
- 6-8 slices of Italian or French bread, about ½ in thick
- 1 cup coarsely grated pecorino cheese (medium aged) or parmesan
- extra virgin olive oil

Slice the eggplant fairly thinly and grill on an iron pan until both sides are brown (about 5 mins on each). You can also use a non-stick pan. The most important thing to remember is to not use any oil. Grill on a dry pan. Place grilled eggplant slices into a dish and season with the extra virgin olive oil.
Toast sliced bread in the oven. Once done, drizzle the bread with olive oil, add the eggplant slices, the pecorino and place in a hot oven so that the cheese melts. Serve immediately and enjoy!
Crostini and Bruschetta are always done in the OVEN and NOT under the grill.

# *Cecina*

## Chickpea savoury cake

Serves 8

- 400 g chickpea flour
- 2 L cold water
- 150 ml extra virgin olive oil
- 1 tsp salt

Slowly sift the flour into the water while mixing with a whisk and keep stirring until you obtain a smooth mixture. Then stir in the oil and salt and set aside for half an hour. Grease a shallow baking tray and pour in the chickpea flour mixture. Bake in a very hot oven until a thin crust is formed. Serve hot.

# *Frittura*

## Fried vegetables

Due to the very high quality of the Tuscan olive oil it is perfect for optimal fried vegetables and meats. You will find them on all menus in a Tuscan restaurant or Trattoria. The type of vegetables in the mixed fry will depend on what is in season. Sage leaves and zucchini flowers are served as antipasto. Artichokes, onion rings, zucchini flowers and strips, mushrooms, peppers are all favourites and can be served either as a side dish or as an antipasto.

## *Pastella per le verdure fritte* 1

### Batter for fried vegetables - Version # 1

Serves 4

- 100 g / ¾ cup of flour
- 1 egg
- half glass of white wine
- water
- 3 Tbs of olive oil
- salt and pepper

Place in a mixing bowl the flour, 1 pinch of salt and pepper, the oil and the egg yolk.
Mix this with the wine and the water until you have a creamy batter. Leave for about half an hour and, when you are about to use it, add the beaten egg white.
Dip your vegetables (eggplant, zucchini, zucchini flowers, onions rings, green tomatoes...) into the batter and fry in hot sunflower oil until browned. Drain on paper towel and serve.

## *Pastella per le verdure fritte* 2

### Batter for fried vegetables - Version # 2

Serves 4

- 100 g flour
- 1 egg yolk
- 80 ml lager beer or sparkling water or white wine
- 1 egg white, whisked with a small pinch of salt until stiff peaks form

Mix flour, egg yolks, salt and beer. You should obtain a creamy mixture.
Let it rest for half an hour then gently fold the egg whites into it.
Dip your vegetables (eggplant, zucchini, zucchini flowers, onions rings, green tomatoes...) into the batter and fry in hot sunflower oil until browned. Drain on paper towel and serve.

# *Pastella per carne*

## Batter for meat

Serves 8

- 200 g potato flour (this must be very, very fine and light)
- 150 g water
- 45 g ice
- 1 pinch of sugar

Unite the potato flour with the sugar, add the water and stir well until the liquid is smooth and creamy , without any lumps from the flour.
Add the ice and leave to cool for 2 minutes for the ice to melt. Stir slightly.
Place the cubes of the meat ( 2-3cms cubes) into the batter, then into the potato flour, then again into the batter.
Use hot peanut oil and place the battered pieces of meat into the oil. It will normally take about 3 or 4 minutes to cook. Take out, drain onto kitchen paper then serve. Add a pinch of salt before serving.

**Why do we use the ice?**
The ice makes the batter cold. When the COLD batter is place into the HOT oil, this is what causes the batter to become crunchy and light without soaking up too much oil.

# *Pastella per carne al vino bianco*

## Batter for meat with white wine

Serves 4

- 150 g flour
- 1 egg
- 1 pinch salt
- ½ glass white wine
- 2 Tbs grappa

In a mixing bowl place the flour and a pinch of salt, the white wine and the grappa. Separate the egg. Leave the egg white to sit for half an hour while you do the rest.
Put the egg yolk (unbeaten at this stage) into the flour/wine mixture. Mix together well with a spoon. Don't beat.
Now we need to beat the egg white until it forms stiff, white peaks, then this needs to be folded into the flour/wine mixture. Place the pieces of meat into the mixture and then into the heated peanut oil.

**How do we get the batter nice and crunchy?**
The oil must be hot but not so hot that it is smoking. Use enough oil so that the meat cubes are immersed in the oil and not touching the bottom or each other.

.............................................................................................................

.............................................................................................................

.............................................................................................................

# *Funghi fritti*

## Fried porcini mushrooms

Serves 4

- 600 g fresh porcini mushrooms
- flour
- salt
- oil for frying

Remove the stalks of the mushrooms and clean the cap and the stalk with a knife. Cut into thin slices, dip into the flour and fry in the boiling oil. Cook for 3 minutes, place on kitchen paper to dry add salt and serve hot. It's important that you don't cook the mushrooms for too long because they will taste bitter. Another tip is to half fry them and then place them on the absorbent paper then just before serving drop them in the oil to heat and crisp, they will be less oily.

# *Salvia fritta*

## Fried sage

Serves 4

- large fresh sage leaves
- 100 g / ¾ cup of flour
- anchovies
- 1 egg
- salt
- 3 tbs of olive oil
- tooth picks

Select the biggest sage leaves. Carefully wash and dry them, placing on some absorbent paper.
Place in a mixing bowl and beat the egg with a pinch of salt , pass the leaves in the egg.
Between 2 leaves add an anchovy fillet and then secure them together with a tooth pick.
Re-pass in the egg mixture then toss in the flour.
Add immediately in the preheated oil, hot enough for fast frying.
Fry very quickly and serve immediately.
For those that don't like archovies you can leave these out of the recipes.

# *Fiori di zucca ripieni e fritti*
## Stuffed and fried zucchini flowers

Serves 4
- 12 zucchini flowers
- 200 g ricotta
- 2 eggs
- 60 g grated parmesan cheese
- flour
- salt and pepper
- oil for fying

Clean well and delicately the zucchini flowers, eliminating the little green leaves at the base and the internal stamen of the flower. Seperate the egg and use one yolk for the filling, add the yolk and mix with the ricotta, parmesan, salt and pepper. Stuff the flowers carefully paying attention to not break the flowers, close and then dust in the flour. Start to heat the oil in a skillet.
Separately beat the remaining egg whites and yolk, pass the floured flowers in the egg batter and then fry in the heated oil. Once golden on both sides, dry on paper, salt lightly and serve hot.

# *Cavolfiore fritto*
## Fried cauliflower

Serves 4
**For the batter: refer to recipe on page 15.**

- 16 cauliflower flowerettes

Blanch the flowerettes in plenty of salted boiling water for 2 minutes from the moment the water comes back to the boil again. Pat the flowerettes dry, pass them through the batter and fry them until golden.

# *Coccoli*

## Bread dough dumplings

Serves 6

- 400 g flour
- 25 g yeast
- 250 ml full cream milk
- a pinch of salt
- frying oil (sun flower or peanut oil)

Dissolve the yeast in the milk. Sift the flour into a bowl, make a well in the middle and pour in the milk. Mix until you obtain a soft, sticky dough. If the dough is too dry, add a little milk. If it is too wet, add a little flour. Cover the dough with a towel or cling film and let it rise in a warm place for a couple of hours. Heat plenty of oil in a deep frypan (the temperature of the oil should be around 160°C). Pinch walnut size pieces from the dough and gently put them in the hot oil and cook until the dumplings are golden. Open one to see if the dumpling is cooked through - if not you might need to lower the temperature of the oil a bit. Once cooked, put the dumplings onto kitchen paper and serve piping hot sprinkled with salt and accompanied by stracchino cheese and/or sliced cold meats (such as prosciutto, ham and salami).

# Tortino di verdure

## Vegetable flans

These dishes can be used as an antipasto, side dishes or some as a first course. In Tuscany a lot of omelettes are also used which can be made with vegetables and eggs alone. They become a “tortino” when flour is added to the mixture.

# Pasta brisee

## Shortcrust pastry

Serves 4-6

- 300 g flour ‘00’
- 150 g butter
- 1 pinch of salt
- 100 ml cold water
- 1 egg

Sieve the flour and the salt onto a flat surface or pasta board. Cut the room temperature butter into smaller cubes and add to the flour, incorporating rapidly with your fingers. Then add little by little the water and beaten egg, kneading rapidly to form a ball of dough. This must be left in the fridge, wrapped in plastic wrap for around 1 hour.
After an hour, on a floured board the dough can be rolled out with a rolling pin and use to line a pie dish for the savoury tart.

# *Torta salata di zucchini*

## Zucchini quiche

Serves 8

- 1 roll of fresh puff-pastry ready made or you can use the 'Pasta Brisee' recipe
- 5-6 zucchinis
- 6  zucchini flowers
- 2 eggs
- 1 cup of fresh cream
- 2 Tbs of grated parmesan
- salt and pepper
- 1 clove of garlic
- finely chopped parsley

In a saucepan heat 3 tablespoons of olive oil with the garlic and some of the chopped parsley. Add the zucchini, chopped into small cubes.
Cook on a live flame continuously moving the saucepan for about 5 minutes. Add salt and pepper as needed. Leave to cool.
Beat the eggs with a pinch of salt, the cream and the parmesan cheese.
Roll out the pastry in a quiche or pie tin, add the zucchini and then cover with the cream/egg mixture.
Add the zucchini flowers in the form of a flower.
Cook in the oven for around 35-40 minutes at 175° C.

# *Torta di pere e gorgonzola*

## Savoury tart with pear and gorgonzola

Serves 4-6

- 1 ready-made puff-pastry sheet
  (you can also use the 'Pasta Brisee' recipe)
- 4 mature pears
- 200 g gorgonzola cheese
- salt and pepper

Preheat oven to 160°C. Spread the pastry into a round quiche pan.
Peel and cut the pears into thin slices.
Using about half of the cheese, place small pieces of the gorgonzola on the pastry base, add the pear slices, then the remainder of the cheese.
Add salt and pepper to taste and cook in the oven for around 40 minutes.

# *'Mezzaluna' di zucchini al pesto*

## Half moon filled with zucchini and fresh pesto

Serves 4

**Pastry:**

- 250 g flour
- 125 g water
- 40 g butter

**Filling:**

- 300 g zucchini
- 100 g of parmesean grated
- 8 Tbs olive oil
- 3 gloves of garlic
- bunch of thyme
- 3 pinches of salt

**Pesto:**

- 4 bunches of fresh basil
- 1 clove of garlic
- 4 Tbs of parmesan cheese
- 1 Tbs of pecorino cheese
- 2 Tbs pine nuts
- 1 cup of olive oil
- 2 pinches of salt
- 1 pinch of white pepper

For the pesto - remove the basil leaves from the stems and place in the blender together with the other ingredients leaving the oil until the end. Mix on low speed for 3 seconds. Put the pesto in a bowl and stir with a wooden spoon. Add more salt and pepper to taste.

For the pastry - mix all ingredients together at the same time, kneading the dough with your hands, and working it as if you were making fresh pasta until you have a smooth, soft ball. Leave to set under a hot saucepan for 30 mins. After this, enlarge the pastry with your hands, then roll out evenly

ON TOP OF A CLEAN TEATOWEL.

Next, wash and cut the zucchini, then sautè in olive oil, 3 pinches of salt, garlic (crushed with the back of a knife) and thyme for about 10 mins on a medium flame (not covered). Let the zucchini mixture cool.

Take the pastry and arrange flat on a surface then place the zucchini mixture on to the dough. Then add on top of the zucchini the pesto. Next roll the pastry and the mixture into a tube shape. Once this has been done, you can then bend gently into a 'Mezzaluna' (half moon) shape. Whisk the egg yolk and then brush lightly over the dough. Place in the oven for 25 minutes at 160 degrees. Serve hot.

# Fiori di zucchini ripieni al forno

## Oven-baked stuffed zucchini flowers

Recipe for 12 flowers

- 12 zucchini flowers
- 2 eggs
- 200 g provola cheese (this is a lightly smoked cheese)
- 1 slice of prosciutto for each flower
- 250 g fresh ricotta
- 3 Tbs parmesan cheese
- pinch of salt
- pepper
- nutmeg
- flour
- sunflower oil for frying

Clean flowers delicately, being careful not to break them. Remove the stamen. Place the flowers on a paper towel to dry.
Dice the provola cheese finely, slice the prosciutto into little strips and combine the ricotta, prosciutto, provola cheese and parmesan together for filling the flowers. Add salt, pepper and the nutmeg to taste.
Heat the oil in a skillet, and in a bowl beat the eggs.
Preheat the oven to medium heat-180°C.

Fill the flowers with the mixture very carefully trying not to break them. Dust them with the flour. Pass the flowers into the eggs and fry them very quickly in the oil.
From the skillet the flowers are placed in a baking dish.

Once all the flowers have been fried lightly and placed in the dish cover with the fresh tomato sauce (be careful not to put too much).
Place in the oven for 10-15mins to warm.

**Alternative:** *You can do the same process above without frying the flowers, and if you do not want to use the tomato sauce you can sprinkle with bread crumbs then place in the oven to heat.*

# *Impasto per pizzettine*

## Dough for little pizzas

Makes 12 little pizzas

- 200 g plain flour
- 1 packet of brewers yeast
- 1 tsp sugar
- 100 ml luke warm water
- 1 pinch of salt

In a large bowl, dissolve the yeast in the luke warm water with the sugar and pinch of salt. Let rest for 5 minutes then add the flour slowly, stirring continuously until you obtain a dough. If the mixture is still too sticky, add some more flour. If it is too dry, add a touch of water. Continue to work the dough with your hands until it becomes smooth. Shape it into a ball and then place in a bowl. Cut a shallow cross into the top, cover it with a cloth and let it rest for 1.5 hours. The dough will rise considerably and tiny bubbles will form on the surface. At this point the dough is ready to be be rolled out to make the pizzas!

# *Pizza Napoletana*

## Neapolitan pizza

Serves 4-6

- ½ kg puréed peeled tomatoes
- 250 g mozzarella
- 5-6 anchovy fillets
- 2 Tbs capers
- 3-4 pinches of oregano

Take the little pizza dough and divide into 3 or 4 pieces. Roll out the dough to form a thin crust one at a time. Then with a cutting round, cut the dough into circles to form your mini pizzas bases. Cover a baking tray with oven paper and lay out the dough. On each mini pizza, put a layer of the tomato, a piece of mozzarella, ½ anchovy fillet and capers and drizzle with olive oil. Place in a hot oven at 200°C for 7-8 minutes, remove and sprinkle with oregano. Your pizzas are ready...and best eaten hot.

# *Pizza rustica patate e rosmarino*

## Potato and rosemary pizza

Serves 2-4

**For the pizza base: see recipe on page 27.**

- 2 potatoes
- olive oil
- rosemary
- salt and pepper

Slice the potatoes thinly and toss them in a little olive oil.
Roll out the pizza dough (made as per the "Little Pizza" recipe) and line 2 lightly oiled pizza trays. Place the potato slices, overlapping each other slightly, onto the pizzas. Sprinkle with rosemary, salt and pepper and bake in a 220°C oven for 10-15 minutes.

# *Pizza margherita*

## Margherita pizza

Serves 4

**For the pizza base: see recipe on page 27.**
**For tomato sauce: see recipe on page 78.**

- 4 balls of buffalo mozzarella
- 12 fresh basil leaves
- salt
- extra virgin olive oil

Take the pizza dough and divide into 3 or 4 equal pieces. Roll out the dough to form a thin pastry base one at a time. Then with a cutting round, cut the dough into circles to form your mini pizza bases. Cover a baking tray with baking paper and lay out the dough. On each mini pizza, place a layer of the tomato sauce (or pureed peeled tomato if you prefer). Slice the buffalo mozzarella balls into thin slices then layer over the pizza. Bake in a 200° oven for 7-8 minutes. Remove and sprinkle torn basil leaves over the top and drizzle with extra virgin olive oil.

# *Torta d'erbe della Lunigiana*

## Lunigiana-style savoury vegetable cake

Serves 4

**For the filling:**

- 600 g spinach with thick part of the stalk removed, thinly sliced
- 600 g silver beet with thick part of the stalk removed, thinly sliced
- 2 leeks, finely sliced
- 2 zucchini, sliced
- 2 eggs
- 2 garlic cloves, finely sliced
- 70 g hard pecorino cheese

Lightly sautè the garlic in the olive oil and add the vegetables. Cook until soft. Mix the vegetables with the pecorino and the eggs in a bowl.

**For the pastry:**

- 300 g flour
- 100 g butter (at room temperature)
- 4 tbs extra virgin olive oil
- 2 egg yolks
- 1 whole egg
- 50 ml water
- salt

Combine all the pastry ingredients in a bowl and mix with your hands until a dough is obtained. Work the dough onto a board for a minute or two, cover it and let it rest for 1 hour. Roll the pastry dough into 2 thin sheets, one bigger than the other. Grease an oven tray and line it with the bigger sheet of pastry, put the vegetable mix in it and cover with the other pastry sheet and secure it. Put in a 180 °C oven and cook for about half an hour.

# *Soufflè ai porcini*

## Porcini soufflè

Serves 4

- 20 g butter
- 20 g flour
- 150 ml milk
- 150 fresh porcini mushrooms, quartered
- 30 g parmesan cheese
- 3 eggs
- salt and pepper
- extra virgin olive oil
- garlic

Pre-heat the oven to 180°C. Melt the butter and add the flour, mixing well. Slowly incorporate the milk and continuously stir until you reach a creamy, smooth but thick consistency. Then, set aside and allow to slightly cool. Take the porcini mushroom pieces and brown them in a little olive oil. Add salt, pepper and garlic to taste. Add the mushroom pieces, 3 egg yolks (keeping the egg whites aside for now), and the parmesan cheese into the creamy mixture you prepared earlier. Mix well, adding any additional salt you feel is necessary. Whisk the egg whites until they stiffen, and fold carefully in to the cream and mushroom mixture. Butter 4 small soufflé dishes and divide the soufflé mixture into each. Allow to cook in the pre-heated oven for 20-30 minutes.

# *Flan di patate e tartufo*

## Light potato flan flavoured with truffles

Serves 16

- 800 g potatoes
- ½ L liquid cream
- 4 eggs and 4 yolks
- 150 g grated parmesan
- 8 Tbs of olive oil
- salt and pepper
- 2 small black truffles

Preheat oven to 160 ° C. Shave the truffles. Peel the potatoes and cut into small cubes, add to saucepan with the olive oil, cover and cook for around 15 minutes. When they are cooked, pass the potatoes through a potatoe masher or better still, a food mill ("passatutto"). Add all ingredients apart from the truffles and mix well with a mixer/food processor until you have a creamy consistency. Then add the shaved truffles.

Butter well a mould (ring moulds are nice for this flan) or make smaller individual portions. Fill ¾ full and cook in a bain-marie for 40 minutes, in a moderate oven.
You can easily create a bain-marie by taking a deep roasting try then placing the small moulds (even disposable aluminium ones) onto the tray, then filling the tray with water to about two-thirds full.

# *Soufflè di parmigiano*

## Parmesan soufflé

Serves 4

- 100 g grated parmesan cheese
- 30 g butter
- 30 g flour
- 250 ml milk
- 4 eggs
- salt and pepper

Butter 4 individual (250 ml) soufflé dishes. Melt the butter in a saucepan. Stir in the flour and cook for a couple of minutes. Slowly incorporate the milk, whilst continuously whisking. Bring to the boil and let simmer for 4 minutes, stirring occasionally. Remove from the heat and add the parmesan. Let it cool slightly then stir in the egg yolks, keep the egg whites aside. Add salt and pepper to taste. Transfer the mixture into a large bowl. In a seperate bowl, beat the egg whites until they slightly stiffen, then fold into the creamy mixture, a third at a time. Fill the individual soufflé dishes with the soufflé mixture. Place them into a pre-heated 180°C oven for approximately 20 minutes. Serve immediately.

# *Sformato di porri*

## Leek flan

Serves 4

You can replace the leeks with zucchini, parmesan, carrots, pumpkin etc

- 75 g of flour
- ¾ L of milk
- 75 g butter
- 3-4 leeks
- 4 eggs
- salt
- pepper
- extra virgin olive oil

Cut the ends of the leeks and discard the green ends. Slice them into thin rings. Heat oil in a skillet and saute the leeks until cooked but not brown.

Next, you make the bechamel sauce.
Over a low heat melt the butter, add the flour and mix with a whisk, keep stirring in the same direction, add the milk slowly and keep stirring.
The mixture will become thick and smooth.
In a food mixer, blend the leeks then stir them into the beschamel sauce with 4 eggs until you obtain a smooth mixture. Place the mixture into small, individual sized moulds. Stand moulds in a baking dish lined with a teatowel, and pour in boiling water to two thirds full. Ensure the teatowel is completely submerged. Bake for about 20 minutes in a pre-heated 170° C oven.

# *Tortino di carciofi*

## Artichoke frittata

Serves 4
- 6 artichokes
- flour
- 6 eggs
- extra virgin olive oil
- 1 lemon
- salt and pepper in grain form
- 1 clove garlic
- parsley

Clean the artichokes, discarding the harder leaves on the exterior, and cut off approximately 2 cm from the top, discarding the pointy end. Cut the artichoke into thin slices of approx 1/2cm and place in a bowl of water and add the juice of 1 lemon.
Dry them after 10 mins with paper towel then toss them in the flour.
In a cake tin or oven pan unite 4 tbsp of oil, the artichokes and the squashed garlic clove, place them in a 170° C oven until they are cooked well though not burnt. Beat the eggs slightly with a pinch of salt. Remove the garlic clove. Place the egg mixture on top of the artichokes and put back into the oven until the eggs are cooked, about 20 minutes.
Add the pepper and a squeeze of lemon juice and garnish with some finely chopped parsley.

# *Cestino di parmigiano*

## Parmesan basket

- Grated Parmesan
- Microwave oven
- A glass with a round base

The amount of grated parmesan will vary depending on the size of the basket you wish to make.

On a sheet of oven paper add a cup of grated parmesan forming an even circle and cook in the microwave for 30 seconds.
As soon as you have taken the cheese out of the microwave allow to cool over the bottom of an overturned glass, making sure that the cheese is on the glass and the paper on the outside. With your hands mould the cheese in to the form of a basket. After 5 minutes carefully peel the baking paper from the glass, lifting the cooled parmesan basket off. It is ready!

This is a wonderful way to serve a mixed salad, you can also add grapes or pieces of pear garnished with balsamic vinegar, which make a very nice combination with the parmesan.

## *Mazzancolle al lardo di Colonnata in puree di ceci*

### Large prawns served with pork fat on a bed of chick pea puree

Serves 5

- 500 g of cooked chick peas
- 10 King prawns ("mazzancolle")
- 10 slices of lard from 'Colonnata'
- rosemary
- salt and pepper to taste
- extra virgin olive oil
- 1 knob of butter

Prepare the mazzancolle by peeling off the shell and removing the vein, leaving the head intact. Sautè the chick peas in olive oil and rosemary and after 5 mins use a mini mixer to blend them into a puree, adding a knob of butter to make the mixture a touch creamier.
Wrap every single "mazzancolla" with a strip of lard, then saute in a non stick pan for 3 minutes.

On a large plate, place a generous amount of the chick pea puree and then place 2 mazzancolle, garnishing with a little rosemary twig.

# *Fritto misto di carne e verdura*

## Fried meat and vegetables

This dish can be served as an antipasto or first course. The meat and vegetables used can be changed according to seasons, and personal preferences.

Serves 6

- 6 lamb chops
- 6 slices of veal
- 3 zucchini
- 3 artichokes
- 6 zucchini flowers
- 3 eggs
- bread crumbs
- flour
- mineral water
- extra virgin olive oil
- salt and pepper
- oil for frying

Beat 2 eggs, add some salt, then pass each piece of meat through the egg mixture, ensuring good coverage. Then dip each piece of meat into the bread crumbs, to ensure an even coating. In another bowl, beat 1 egg, 3 spoonfuls of flour, a spoonful of oil, half a glass of mineral water, salt an pepper. Into this mixture, add the zucchini, sliced into long strips, along with the zucchini flowers. Clean the artichokes, cut into spears and coat in the flour.

In a large, deep frypan, add the olive oil and heat. Once it is hot, add the meat, cooking slowly to ensure the meat cooks all the way through.

Towards the end of the cooking process, add in the vegetables. Remove the meat and vegetables from the oil and strain on some absorbant paper to remove excess oil. Sprinkle with salt and then serve hot!

# *Primi Piatti*

## First Courses

# *Panzanella*

## Bread and vegetable salad

Serves 6

- 400 g  2-day-old Tuscan-style bread, sliced
- 4 tomatoes, diced
- 2 red onions or 4 spring onions, sliced thinly
- 1 cucumber, finely sliced
- 10 basil leaves, ripped in half
- 2 Tbs red wine vinegar
- 100 ml extra virgin olive oil
- 2 pinches of salt
- 2 pinches of pepper

Soak the bread in cold water for a few minutes. Then squeeze out as much water as you can, crumble the bread in a big bowl, add all the vegetables and basil leaves and mix well. Add half of the olive oil, salt and pepper and mix again. Allow to stand in the fridge for an hour or more. Add the vinegar and remaining extra virgin olive oil and mix again. Serve, garnishing with basil leaves.

# *Ribollita*

## Tuscan bread and vegetable soup

Serves 6

- 300 g 2-day-old Tuscan-style bread, finely sliced
- 300 g dried cannellini beans
- 2 bunches black-leaf kale, remove the thick part of the stalk and slice thinly
- ½ a savoy cabbage, remove the hard bottom part of the core and slice thinly
- 1 bunch silver beet, remove the thick part of the stalk and slice thinly
- 1 red onion, thinly sliced
- 1 garlic clove, chopped
- 1 Tbs of tomato concentrate, diluted in a little warm water
- 2 celery stalks, sliced
- 2 carrots, halved and sliced
- 2 potatoes, halved and sliced
- 8 Tbs extra virgin olive oil
- salt and pepper

Put the cannellini beans in a pot. Add one and a half litres of water, 2 tbs of olive oil, 2 garlic cloves, a couple of sage leaves, salt and a few peppercorns. Cover with a lid and place over a very low flame. The water must simmer gently and not boil. The beans will take 2 to 3 hours to cook. With a slotted spoon take out ¼ of the beans and puree the rest. Sautè the garlic and onion in a pot and when the onion softens, add the tomato concentrate. Add all the vegetables except the beans and cook for a few minutes. Then add the pureed beans and cook until all the vegetables are soft (for around 45 minutes). Add the whole beans, bread, salt and pepper and stir well. Cook for a further 5 minutes then cover and set aside for 15 minutes. Serve with a drizzle of extra virgin olive oil and make sure there is freshly ground pepper on the table. This soup is even better if it is reheated the next day - ribollita (which means "reboiled") gets its name from the fact that it is reboiled and improves with reboiling.

# *Carabaccia*

## Tuscan onion soup

Serves 4

- 1 kg onion, sliced finely
- 1 celery stalk, diced
- 1 carrot, diced
- 4 slices of unsalted Tuscan-style crusty bread
- 8 Tbs olive oil
- salt and ground pepper
- 1 ¼ L vegetable broth
- grated pecorino cheese (sheep cheese)

Sautè the onions, celery stalk and carrot in the olive oil. When the onion is soft add the boiling broth and cook on a low heat for about 40 minutes. Add salt and pepper to taste. Toast the bread and place a slice into each bowl. Pour the soup onto each slice of bread and garnish wtih plenty of grated pecorino.

"Carabaccia" is the name of a type of barge that was used to transport salt and sand from one side of Florence's Arno river to the other. The name was given to this soup recipe which emerged from the Renaissance kitchen of the Medici family.

When Catherine de Medici moved to France to marry the son of a French King, she took along the Carabaccia recipe, which later became the famous French onion soup, *Soupe à l'oignon.*

# *Pappa al pomodoro*

## Thick tomato and bread soup

Serves 4

- 300 g 2-day-old Tuscan-style bread, finely sliced
- 500 g ripe peeled tomatoes
- 3 - 4 garlic cloves, crushed
- optional 1 – 2 dried chillies, crushed
- 10 basil leaves ripped
- 1 L vegetable stock
- extra virgin olive oil
- 1 tsp of salt
- ground black pepper

Remove the core and cut a cross into the skin of both ends of the tomatoes then place the tomatoes in abundant boiling water for a couple of minutes. Strain, then rinse them in very cold water and peel. Sautè the garlic in 8 tbs of olive oil until it is lightly coloured (if you are going to use them, add the chillies too). Add the tomatoes, salt and pepper to the pot and cook for 10 minutes. Add the boiling stock and bread. Cook for a further 10 minutes, stirring often. Cover and let the soup rest for twenty minutes. Add the basil and 100 ml of olive oil, stir well and serve.
The soup should be very thick and warm, not hot.

# *Zuppa di farro*

## Spelt soup

This unusual soup has a very thick and creamy consistency. It is hearty and extremely nutritious, and is a perfect meal for the end of gray winter day. 'Garfagnana' is the area in Tuscany which is famous for its farro.

- 3 Tbs olive oil
- 200 g spelt
- 200 g dried white beans, such as Cannellini or Borlotti; dried beans need to be soaked overnight or at least 12 hours
- 1 cup each of roughly chopped onion, celery and carrot
- 3 cloves garlic, chopped
- 1 large can whole tomatoes
- chopped fresh sage and fresh rosemary to taste
- salt and pepper to taste
- 100 g pancetta / salted pork / bacon (optional)

An optional non vegetarian choice would be to brown 4 ounces or 100 grams of pancetta, prosciutto or salt pork in olive oil before adding the chopped vegetables. When the meat is lightly browned, add the onion, carrots and celery and sauté until fairly soft and golden. When the vegetables are lightly browned, add the chopped garlic and continue to sauté until the garlic just begins to colour.

Add the soaked beans, the spelt, and the canned tomatoes. Then cover all the ingredients in boiling water, to about 1 inch above the barley mixture. Let the mixture then boil gently for at least 1 hour, until the soup has reached a creamy consistency. At this point, add the fresh herbs and the salt and pepper. Continue to cook for just a few minutes to blend these flavours. Some cooks of the Garfagnana believe that the soup is best served on the second day, after the flavours have had a chance to blend even more, and the spelt has further softened; you be the judge.

In Garfagnana, it is not uncommon for cooks to add a piece of smoked or salted pigskin to the soup as it boils. Knowing that this might not be available to all our cooks, we suggest the alternative pork products of pancetta, prosciutto or salt pork.

# *Gnocchi di patate con pesto alla fornaia*

## Potato gnocchi with walnut pesto sauce

Serves 6

**For the Sauce:**

- 4 bunches of basil, leaves only
- 80 g shelled walnuts
- 2 garlic cloves
- 8 Tbs grated pecorino cheese
- 200 ml extra virgin olive oil
- 1 pinch of salt
- 1 pinch of ground pepper
- the juice of ¼ of a lemon

Mix all the ingredients except the pecorino cheese in a food processor until you obtain a smooth mixture then stir in the pecorino cheese.

**For the dough:**

- 1 kg potatoes
- 300 g Italian "00" or plain flour
- salt
- 1 egg

Boil the potatoes whole and unpeeled in plenty of water until tender (on average 40 minutes should be long enough). Drain and peel them while still very hot. Put them through a food mill and mill them directly onto a bench. Sift the flour on top of them, make a well in the middle and break the egg into the well. Mix gently to achieve a soft dough. Add more flour if the dough is too wet. Roll the dough into long logs of about 2 cm diameter then cut them into 5 cm long pieces. Flour them to prevent sticking and cook them in a pot with abundant salted boiling water. Cook a few of them at a time. The gnocchi will be cooked after about a minute after they have floated to the surface. Drizzle them with pesto as you put them on the serving dish and serve immediately.

*Alternative: Gnocchi can be served wth a wide array of different sauces. Please refer to our 'sauces' section for some other options.*

# *Gnocchi di polenta al sugo di carne*

## Polenta gnocchi with meat sauce

Serves 6 - 8

**For the meat sauce:**

- 1 onion, chopped finely
- 1 carrot, chopped finely
- 1 celery stalk, chopped finely
- 5 stalks of parsley, chopped finely
- 100 ml extra virgin olive oil
- 400 g minced beef
- 1 pork sausage, skinned and chopped
- 1 glass dry red wine
- Optional: 25 g dried porcini mushrooms, soaked and chopped
- 400 g tomatoes, peeled and chopped
- 2 ladles meat stock
- 1 tsp salt

Sautè the vegetables in the oil until lightly golden. Add the mince and the sausage. Cook and stir until browned. Add the wine and stir until it evaporates. Add the tomatoes, stock and salt. Let it simmer for a couple of hours. If it dries out, add a little stock or water. At the end of the cooking process check if there is enough salt and adjust to taste.

**For the gnocchi:**

- 700 g polenta (corn meal)
- 2 L water or stock
- a pinch salt
- a pinch black ground pepper

Boil the water or the stock with salt and pepper and slowly pour the polenta into the liquid, whisking continuously. Keep stirring and cook for about 20 minutes. Pour the polenta onto a tray and spread it until you obtain a thickness of about 2 cm. Let it cool. When the polenta is set, cut it into discs and toss them through the hot meat sauce. Serve.

*Alternative – Gnocchi can be served wth a wide array of different sacues. Please refer to our 'sauces' section for some other options.*

# *Gnocchi di semolino*

## Semola gnocchi

- 250 g semola flour
- 1 L of milk
- 2 eggs
- 20 g butter
- 2 Tbs parmesan
- pinch of salt

Heat milk with the salt, when milk boils, add the semola, stirring constantly. Cook for 5 mins and then remove from the heat, let cool then add the eggs, butter and parmesan and mix well.

Place the semola dough between 2 sheets of grease proof baking paper and roll out with a rolling pin until it is about 1/2 cm thick. Remove the top layer of paper and with a pasta stamp or even the rim of a champagne flute or normal glass you can make the round shapes.
Take a pyrex dish, grease with a bit of butter, then place the gnocchi, overlapping slightly to cover the bottom of the dish.

At this point you have a couple of choices:
1 – Simple. Top with butter and grated parmesan and bake in a hot oven for 10-12 minutes.
2 - Top with butter, grated parmesan and bechamel sauce and bake in hot oven for 10-12 minutes.
3 – Butter, grated truffle and a little parmesan and bake as above. If you like truffles, you can also add when you remove from heat and add the butter and parmesan for a stronger flavour.
4 – You can also top with a tomato sauce (see recipe), meat sauce (see recipe), sauce made with porcini mushrooms (see recipe) spinach and bechamel... the options are endless!

# *Gnudi con burro e salvia*

## Ricotta and spinach dumplings with butter and sage

Serves 4

- 400 g ricotta
- 500 g spinach with the thick part of the stalk removed
- 2 eggs
- 3 Tbs flour
- a pinch of nutmeg
- a pinch of salt
- a pinch of ground lack pepper
- 4 Tbs grated parmesan cheese
- 8 sage leaves
- 100 g butter

Wash the spinach twice, place it in a pot with the lid on and cook it until its volume is reduced you do not need to add water. Let it cool down, wring it out either by hand or using a clean teatowel and chop it finely. Mix the spinach with the ricotta cheese, eggs, flour, parmesan cheese, salt, pepper and nutmeg until you obtain a smooth mixture. If the mixture is too wet add in a bit more flour. Flour your hands. Form balls a bit larger than the size of a walnut with the mixture. Cook a few gnudi at a time in plenty of boiling salted water. When they float, allow them to boil for another 2 minutes, then gently catch them with a strainer and put them on a serving dish. Melt the butter with the sage without cooking the butter, adding a little water to prevent from burning. Dash the gnudi with the butter and sage sauce, sprinkle with extra parmesan cheese and serve.

# *Pasta fresca*

## Fresh pasta

Both fresh and dried pasta should be cooked 'al dente', tender but chewy. Most people overcook their pasta and don't put enough (if any!!) salt in the water. Use a **LARGE** pot that is big enough to let the pasta float freely during cooking. Bring the water to a full rolling boil, salt it **GENEROUSLY**, and then add the pasta. As soon as the water returns to a boil start timing the pasta and stirring during the boil to prevent it sticking together. The time will vary depending on the pasta though fresh pasta usually takes from 2-4 minutes depending on the thickness and for dried pasta it usually takes about 8-12 minutes. For any stuffed pasta such as ravioli you may wish to remove them from the boiling water with a slotted spoon instead of tipping into a colander as they are more delicate.

This is the base recipe for all pastas:

Serves 4

- 400 g of flour
- 4 eggs
- 4 Tbs of white wine - optional
- pinch of salt

On a work surface, preferably wooden, build the flour in a mound and make a well in its center. Break the eggs into the well and then add in the wine and the salt.

With a fork, lightly beat the eggs. Then in a circular motion, gradually incorporate flour from the sides of the well until combined.

With the heel of your hand knead the dough pushing it down and away and turning it repeatedly using a dough scraper if it sticks and continue until it is smooth and elastic for at least 15 -20 minutes. If it sticks to the surface or seems a little soft, sprinkle it with flour. Gather dough into a ball.

For hand-made pasta without the pasta machine, see below:

The next step is to decide on the preferred type of pasta such as lasagne,

tagliatelle, ravioli, etc, roll it out (for noodle pasta see below) and buon appetito!

For noodle pasta, rolling and forming pasta:

On a clean surface dusted with flour, flatten the kneaded dough with your hand. With a flour-dusted rolling pin, roll it out to desired thickness according to how you wish to use the pasta.
Loosely roll up the pasta around the rolling pin and unroll onto a flour-dusted kitchen towel, leaving it until dry to the touch but still flexible, about 10 minutes or less if the air is dry.
On the work surface, roll the pasta into a cylinder. With a small sharp knife, cut crosswise into ribbons of desired width.

## *Abbinamento: paste e salse*

### Matching pasta to sauce

**Shaped Pasta** Examples: Conchiglie, farfalle, fusilli, gemelli, gnocchetti, gramigna, lumache, lumaconi, orecchiette, radiatori, route, rotini, and trenne Sauce: Thick tomato sauces, meat sauces, chunky sauces, and cheese sauces. **Tubular Pasta** Examples: Canneroni, cannolicchi, cavatappi, garganelli, macaroni, maccheroncelli, manicotti, paccheri, penne, rigatoni, tortiglioni, and ziti Sauce: Thick tomato sauces, meat sauces, chunky sauces, and thick cream sauces **Strand Pasta** Examples: Angel hair, capellini, chitarra, fedelini, spaghetti, and vermicelli Sauce: Light tomato sauces, butter based sauces, light oil based sauces, and light cream based sauces. **Ribbon Pasta** Examples: Fettuccine, lasagne, linguine, pappardelle, riginette, tagliatelle, and trenette Sauce: For the wider dried pastas - meat sauces, thick tomato sauces, and thick cream sauces. For narrow or fresh pastas - Light tomato sauces, butter based sauces, light oil based sauces, and light cream based sauces. **Soup Pasta** Examples: Acini di pepe, alphabets, anellini, conchigliette, ditali, farfalline, orzo, pastine, risi, stele, stortini, and tubetti Sauce: Light sauces, mainly used in broth or soups with a light base. **Stuffed Pasta** Examples: Agnolotti, pansotti, ravioli, tortelli, and tortellini Sauce: Light tomato sauce, light cream based sauce, and broth.

## *Sapori e colori della pasta*

### Flavours and colours of pasta

Ingredients added to the pasta dough

**Spinach** - Finely chopped spinach is added to the pasta dough according to the recipe instructions. Light green.
**Broccoli** - Finely chopped broccoli is added to the pasta dough according to the recipe instructions. Mild broccoli flavour. Medium to dark green.
**Tomato -** Tomato paste is added to the pasta dough according to the recipe instructions. Mild tomato flavour. Light reddish-orange to dark reddish-orange.

**Beets** - Cooked beets, which are used mostly to add colour, are pureed and strained, then added to the pasta dough according to the recipe instructions. Deep pink to dark red.

**Carrot** - Pureed carrots or carrot juice is added to the pasta dough according to the recipe instructions. Strong carrot taste orange in colour.

**Red Bell Pepper** - Roasted bell peppers are pureed and added according to the recipe instructions. Slightly sweet. Bright orangish-red.

**Chili Pepper** - Different varieties of chili peppers, such as jalapeño, cayenne, poblano, and Serrano, can be used for chili pepper pasta. The peppers should have the seeds removed and then be chopped into fine pieces or pureed. Dried chili peppers are also used. The flavour will vary in strength according to the degree of hotness of the variety of chili pepper used. Colour will vary according to the variety of pepper used.

**Squid Ink** - Squid or cuttlefish ink is strained from the eye "bags or sacs" of the squid or cuttlefish. It is added to the pasta recipe for a unique flavour and colour. Mild seafood flavour Dark gray, almost black in colour.

**Garlic** - Crushed garlic cloves are added according to the recipe instructions. Garlic taste Creamy beige colour.

**Garlic and Herbs** - Crushed garlic cloves and one or more herbs, such as sage, thyme, parsley, chives, rosemary, tarragon, basil, and oregano, are added to the pasta dough. Spicy garlic flavour Creamy beige in colour with green flecks.

**Curry** - Curry powder, which is a spice blend that is generally composed of cumin, turmeric, coriander, ground red pepper, and cloves, is added to the pasta dough to provide a distinct flavour Spicy. Tint of burnt orange.

**Saffron** - Saffron is added to pasta dough to give it a distinct flavour and colour. Spicy, mildly bitter Bright yellowish-gold in colour.

**Lemon** - Lemon pasta contains lemon juice and/or lemon zest, which provides a very mild lemon flavour to the pasta. Mildly tart, lemon taste. Light yellow.

**Strawberry** - The strawberries are simmered to soften them and then the juice is strained from the strawberries and added to the pasta dough. Dull pale red colour.

**Chocolate** - Unsweetened cocoa powder and sugar are added to the dough to give it a mildly sweet chocolate flavour. It works well in sweet pasta dishes. Mild chocolate brown tone.

# *Ravioli ricotta e spinaci*

## Ricotta and spinach ravioli

Serves 6

**For the Pasta: refer to recipe on page 48.**

**For the filling:**

- 300 g fresh sheep ricotta cheese
- 800 g spinach with the thick part of the stalk removed
- 6 Tbs grated parmesan cheese
- 1 egg
- a pinch of nutmeg
- a pinch of salt

Wash the spinach twice and cook it using just the water left on the leaves from the rinsing. Squeeze it well.
Let the spinach cool down, then mix the ricotta and grated parmesan, egg, salt, and nutmeg and mix well until you obtain a smooth mixture.

**For the sauce:**

- 3 Tbs butter
- 6 sage leaves
- a small pinch of salt
- a small pinch of ground black pepper

Melt the butter with the sage. Add a little of the pasta water to prevent from burning and to elongate the sauce.

Roll the dough through a pasta machine until it is very thin (about 0.5 mm thick). Cut into long 5 cm-wide strips and put small spoonfuls of the ricotta and spinach filling along the strips at a regular intervals about 5 cm apart. Moisten the edges of the pasta and between the fillings with a damp pastry brush. Place another strip on top and press around each mound of filling with your fingertips to seal well. Cut into squares with a pastry wheel cutter. Cook the ravioli in plenty of boiling salty water in batches (cook for about 2 minutes after the water returns to the boil).

Drain them with a slotted spoon and place them on a platter, pour the melted butter over, sprinkle with parmesan cheese and serve immediately.

# *Ravioli ripieni di noci e melanzane*

## Eggplant and walnut ravioli

Serves 6

**For the Pasta: refer to recipe on page 48.**

**For the Filling:**

- 300 g fresh sheep ricotta cheese
- 6 Tbs grated parmesan
- 2 eggs
- salt and pepper
- 2 large eggplants
- 100 g shelled walnuts
- 1 cup of hot water

Peel the eggplants and cut into slices of about 1 cm thick. Heat a frypan with a thin layer of salt covering the bottom. Do not add oil, only the salt. When the frypan is hot add the slices of eggplant and grill until they are light brown. Place on a plate and cover with a drizzling of olive oil.

With a kitchen aid or a blender crush the walnuts with the eggplant, ricotta, parmesan, salt and pepper to form a creamy filling. Do this QUICKLY, don't over process.
You need to do this just enough so that the ingredients blend together but not too much!

Roll the fresh pasta very thinly on a pasta board (or similar surface) and place teaspoons of the mixture in a line about 5-6 cms apart.
Fold over the half of the pasta without the mixture onto the other half that is holding the ricotta/eggplant mixture.
With your finger press down firmly between each 'mound' and then use the pasta cutter to separate each ravioli.

In a large frypan melt the butter with 10 fresh sage leaves, then add ½ ladle of the pasta water.
The water is added to prevent the butter from burning and helps it 'cling' to the pasta.

When the ravioli are cooked gently remove from the water with a large strainer (never tip out into a spaghetti strainer as they will break) and add to the frypan with the butter/sage. Sautè together for about 2 mins. Place on the plates, sprinkle with grated parmesan and black pepper.
If you like truffles this is the time to also grate onto the ravioli!
Fantastico!

**Alternative:** *You can substitute the eggplant and walnuts for artichokes (as for the carciofi trifolati recipe on page 124) to make "Artichoke ravioli".*

# *Ravioli di zucca e amaretti*

## Pumpkin ravioli with amaretti cookies

Serves 6

**For the Pasta: refer to recipe on page 48.**

**For the filling:**

- 1 small pumpkin 500 g
- 3 amaretti cookies
- 2/3 cup minced candied fruit (optional)
- 2/3 cup freshly ground parmesan cheese
- salt and freshly ground pepper
- freshly ground nutmeg

**For the sauce:**

- ½ cup butter
- a handful of fresh sage leaves
- 1 cup fresh parmesan

Preheat the oven to approxmately 200°C and bake the whole pumpkin for around 50 minutes or until tender. With a rolling pin break the amaretti biscuits into small pieces.
Cut the pumpkin in half and scoop out the flesh discarding the seeds. Mix the pulp of the pumpkin with the amaretti's, candied fruit, parmesan cheese, nutmeg salt salt and pepper to taste and mix well.

Roll the fresh pasta very thinly on a pasta board (or similar surface) and place teaspoons of the mixture in a line about 5-6 cms apart.
Fold over the half of the pasta without the mixture onto the other half that is holding the mixture. With your finger press down firmly between each 'mound' and then use the pasta cutter to separate each ravioli.

Boil a large pot of water, add a handful of salt and then the ravioli, they should rise to the top in only a few minutes. In the meantime melt the butter and sage in a frypan being careful not to brown the butter. Add a half ladle of the water from the pasta to the butter as this prevents the butter from burning and elongates the sauce. Let the sauce reduce for a minute or two. When the ravioli are cooked add them to the frypan and toss in the butter being careful not to break them, serve immediately with fresh sprinkling of parmesan and ground pepper.

# *Ravioli di patate alla Mugellana*

## Potato ravioli from Mugello

Serves 6

**For the Pasta: refer to recipe on page 48.**

**Recipe for the Filling:**

- 600g white potatoes (not watery)
- 100 g pancetta o bacon
- 6 Tbs grated parmesan cheese
- 2 eggs
- salt and pepper
- 2 garlic cloves
- rosemary
- nutmeg
- olive oil

In a saucepan slightly boil the potatoes and let cool, peel and strain through a sieve.

Sautè lightly the finely chopped pancetta, garlic and a little fresh rosemary on a sprig. As soon as the garlic begins to change colour remove with the rosemary. Place the potatoes in a bowl together with the pancetta, oil, add 2 eggs, 4 tablespoons of parmesan, a little nutmeg, salt and pepper, stir well and leave to stand.

Roll out the pasta, place the mixture onto the pasta, add a top layer of pasta, then seal with your fingers and cut either with a knife or a pasta cutter.

Boil the water, add a generous handful of salt and cook the ravioli, normally around 2-3 minutes. Remove gently from the water using a large slotted spoon to prevent breakage.

These are wonderful served with a ragu sauce, either meat, duck, rabbit, hare or pheasant.

Serve immediately and sprinkle with fresh parmesan.

# *Maccheroni Senesi al sugo di carne*

## Ribbon pasta typical of Siena served with meat sauce

Serves 6-8

**For the pasta: refer to recipe on page 48.**

**For the meat sauce: refer to recipe on page 79.**

Cut the pasta sheets into 2 pieces. Take one pasta sheet and flour it. Starting at one end fold it in 10 cm even folds until the whole sheet is folded. Cut the folded pasta in 2 cm wide slices. Unroll the slices, flour them lightly to prevent them from sticking to one another. Cook the pasta in plenty of boiling salted water (about 1 litre for 100 g of pasta and about a tbs of salt for every 400 g of pasta). Cooking time varies according to the pasta thickness but on average is 4 minutes. Toss the pasta through the sauce and put on a platter. Serve immediately.

# *Pici con le briciole*

## Typical ribbon pasta from Siena with a traditional breadcrumb sauce

Serves 6

**For the sauce:**

- About 300 g Tuscan-style bread, sliced, toasted lightly and crumbed with your hands
- 4 - 5 garlic cloves, chopped finely
- 3 anchovy fillets, chopped finely
- extra virgin olive oil
- salt
- black pepper
- hard, aged pecorino cheese (sheep cheese)

Sautè the garlic and the bread crumbs in a generous amount of olive oil until the bread crumbs are crispy. Then add the anchovies, salt and black pepper, toss and set aside.

**For the pasta:**

- 500 g plain flour
- 1 egg
- about 250 ml lukewarm water
- 1 pinch of salt

For the pasta, in a bowl, make a well in the flour and start to incorporate the egg, the lukewarm water and salt until a firm dough is obtained. Work the dough until it is smooth and then let it rest for at least an hour, covering it with a tea towel. To form the pici, pinch the dough with your finger to take a hazelnut-sized ball of it then roll it and stretch it on the bench until you obtain a long uneven thick spaghetti. Cook the pici in abundant salted water then toss them in a pan through the sauce. Serve with grated pecorino cheese.

# *Pici all'Aglione*
## Garlic & Tomato sauce

**For the sauce:**
- 6 large garlic cloves
- 1 kilo of mature tomatoes
- seasoned Pecorino cheese
- extra Virgin Olive Oil
- 1 whole peperoncino
- salt

Crush the garlic cloves with the back of a knife and place in abundant olive oil over low heat to avoid burning the garlic and spoil the sauce making it bitter. When the garlic is golden break about the peperoncino and add both the seeds and the chopped skin to the pan. Add the chopped tomatoes, making sure to remove the seeds first. Add a pinch of salt (or to taste) and allow to simmer on a low flame until the sauce is thick and well seasoned. As soon as the 'pici' are cooked drain them and add to the saucepan to sauté lightly together.

# *Lasagna tradizionale di carne*
## Traditional lasagna

**Pasta: refer to recipe on page 48.**
**Meat Ragu: refer to recipe on page 79.**
**Bechamel sauce: refer to recipe on page 83.**

You will need to cut the prepared pasta into sheets to fit the size of the pyrex dish. The pasta sheets will need to be cooked in boiling, well salted water for 2 mins. Drain the pasta sheets.
Take a large, square or rectangular pyrex dish, making the first layer with the meat sauce. The second layer will be the pasta sheets, then cover again with meat sauce and then with beschiamella and a handful of grated parmesan cheese. Repeat this for 3 or 4 layers or until you use all of the ingredients. You will finish with meat sauce and bechamel. Don't sprinkle parmesan on this layer as it will burn in the oven.
Cook for 30 mins in a hot oven of around 180° C.

# *Lasagna ai carciofi*

## Artichoke lasagna

Serves 6 - 8

**Pasta: refer to recipe on page 48.**

**Arichoke: refer to recipe on page 124.**

**Bechamel sauce: refer to recipe on page 83.**

Take a large, square or rectangular pyrex dish making the first layer with the artichokes. The second layer will be the pasta sheets, then cover again with artichokes and then with bechamel and a handful of grated parmesan cheese. Repeat this for 3 or 4 layers or until you use all of the ingredients. You will finish with the artichokes and the bechamel.
Don't sprinkle parmesan on this layer as it will burn in the oven.
Cook for 30 mins in a hot oven of around 180° C.

# *Spaghetti alle vongole*

## Spaghetti with clams

Serves 4

- 1 kg clams, washed thoroughly to eliminate any traces of sand
- 350 g spaghetti
- basil leaves, ripped
- 100 g cherry tomatoes, quartered
- 2 garlic cloves, chopped finely
- 2 dried red chili peppers, crushed
- ½ glass of dry white wine

Sautè lightly garlic and chillies in olive oil then add the clams and wine and cover with a lid. When the clams have opened up, add the 'al dente' spaghetti cooked in abundant salted water, the cherry tomatoes and the basil and toss. Serve immediately.

# *Risotto e brodo*

## Risotto and broth

**How do we use the various types of broth?**

Different broths are used depending on what type of risotto you would like to cook. The broth 'creates' the dish and can also be used in stews, to flavour larger cuts of meat, fish and even cooking with fruit.
You can also make a clear broth to 'drink', like a consommè.

There are 3 principal types of 'brodo' (meat), 'fumetto' (made from fish) and vegetable broth.

The broth made from meats such as lamb, beef, veal and chicken are the most universal and we can use them to flavour stews and the world famous risotto. Practically all types of risotto are made using the meat broth, excluding those with fish, fruit and champagne.

For risotto made with fruit eg- strawberries, orange, figs or pear and gorgonzola, we use a lighter vegetable broth which is much more delicate and allows the taste of the fruit to come through.

For risotto made with champagne we use the broth made with meat but very diluted in the proportion of ½ litre of meat broth to 1–1.5 litres of water. You will then have 2 litres of broth.

For all types of risotto using seafood we always use 'fumetto'.

If instead you would like to make consommè then we use the clarified broth, derived from the meat broth.

# *Brodo di verdure*

## Vegetable broth

- 1 medium onion, white or red
- ⅓ of a leek
- 1 mature tomato
- 3 carrots
- 2 sticks of celery
- 2 bay leaves
- 1 Tbs of black pepper corns, smashed
- 6 juniper berries
- 1 Tbs of large rock salt
- 5 L of water
- ½ cup of olive oil
- 1 sprig of parsley

Cut the vegetables in large pieces and add to a large pan of cold water, then add a good handful of rock salt, the juniper berries and crushed peppercorns. Take the onion, cut in half and BURN in a hot saucepan WITHOUT oil or butter. This caramelizes the onion and brings out the sweetness. Add to the water, cover and leave on a low flame to simmer for about 2 hours.
After 2 hours, take out the large remaining pieces of vegetables, then strain through a metal strainer.
This recipe can be used as a base for soups, risotto, sauces.
You can also freeze broth and reheat to use at a later date.

# *Brodo di carne vitello, manzo o pollo*

## Meat broth: Veal, Beef or Chicken

- 200 g of beef with the fat (or Veal for veal broth)
- 1-2 bones with marrow
  or: veal for veal broth (preferably "Ossobuco" veal shank)
  or: chicken for chicken broth
- 3 carrots
- 1 medium onion, white or red
- 2 sticks of celery
- 2 bay leaves
- 1 Tbs of black pepper corns, smashed
- 6 juniper berries
- 1 Tbs of rock salt
- 5 L of water
- ½ cup of olive oil
- 1 sprig of parsley

Cut the vegetables in large pieces and add to the large pan of cold water along with the meat/bones, then add a good handful of rock salt, the juniper berries and crushed peppercorns. Take the onion, cut in half and BURN in a hot saucepan WITHOUT oil or butter. This caramelizes the onion and brings out the sweetness. Add to the water, cover and leave on a low flame to simmer for about 2 hours.
After 2 hours, take out the large remaining pieces of vegetables and meat, then strain through a metal strainer.
This recipe can be used as a base for soups, risotto, sauces. You can also freeze broth and reheat to use at a later date.

**For Chicken broth:**
Substitute the beef for chicken and follow the above instructions.

# Brodo di pesce o 'Fumetto'
## Fish broth

- 1 kg of fish bones (not salmon or sardines)
- 1 celery stalk
- 1 carrots
- 1leek
- 1 white onion
- 3 garlic cloves
- 1 glass of dry white wine
- bunch of parsley
- 10 white peppercorns
- 1 handful of rock salt
- 3 L of cold water
- 4 tbsp olive oil

Wash the bones very well and remove any blood. Any remaining fish meat can be left. Cut the vegetables into chunky pieces. In a large saucepan place the vegetables, bones, salt, pepper and the crushed garlic (not chopped but crushed with the back of a knife) with 1.5 litre of water and the glass of white wine. The peppercorns will need to be crushed in the same way before placing in the water. Cover, lower the flame and simmer together for 1.5 hours. You can use this broth for risotto, soups, stews and also to cook  the pasta when you are making fish recipes.

# *Risotto di base*

## Basic risotto

Serves 4

- 320 g Arborio rice
- 1 white onion, small
- 2 Tbs butter
- 200 g parmesan
- 2 - 3 L boiling beef /other stock
- 1 cup dry white wine
- 3 Tbs olive oil

Thinly slice the onion and sauté in the oil with 1 tablespoon of butter. It is at this point that you would add any of the vegetables or meat such as pancetta to the saucepan, with the onion.

After around 5-6 minutes as soon as the onion is translucent, add the rice, a good pinch of salt and allow to 'toast' over a high heat for about 2–4 minutes stirring constantly. The rice will absorb all of the flavours of the vegetables or meat before the actual cooking begins and the rice absorbs the broth.

Now, add the white wine and once it evaporates add in the **boiling** broth a little at a time. (It is CRUCIAL that the broth is added when it is boiling or very hot otherwise the rice will become 'gluggy'). Stir occasionally making sure that the rice never becomes too dry.
Continue to gradually add small amounts of the boiled broth allowing each addition to be absorbed before adding the next. Stir it from time to time keeping the rice from sticking to the bottom of the pan.
Use a medium heat and cook slowly uncovered.
After 15-20 minutes the rice will be cooked. Remove from heat and add the remaining butter, parmesan and stir through the rice well (in Italian, 'mantecare').
Cover and leave to stand 2-4 minutes. Serve hot.

# *Risotto di parmgiano e zafferano*

## Parmesan and saffron risotto

Serves 4

- 5 Tbs grated parmesan cheese
- a generous pinch of Saffron stems

Follow the recipe for 'Basic Risotto'. 5 minutes before you turn off the heat, add the saffron and grated parmesan cheese. Stir through the rice well (in Italian, "mantecare"). Cover and leave to stand 2–4 minutes. Serve hot.

# *Risotto con le zucchine*

## Zucchini risotto

Serves 4

- 320 g arborio rice
- 2-3 zucchinis
- 50 g pancetta, diced into small cubes
- 50 ml extra virgin olive oil
- 1 white onion
- a handful of parsely, chopped finely
- 1 L vegetable or chicken broth
- 3 Tbs parmesan cheese
- 30 g butter
- salt and pepper

Cut the zucchini lengthwise and slice them. Sautè the onion, garlic and pancetta in the olive oil. Add the zucchini, salt and pepper and cook on a high flame. When the zucchini is lightly golden, add the rice. Mix well. Add the boiling broth bit by bit and cook on a low heat for around 15 minutes. Remove from heat and add the remaining butter, parmesan and parsley. Stir through the rice well (in Italian, "mantecare").
Cover and leave to stand 2–4 minutes. Serve hot.

# *Risotto di pere e gorgonzola*

## Pear and gorgonzola risotto

Serves 4

- 320 g Arborio rice
- 2 Tbs butter
- 2 scallions (spring onions)
- 2-3 L boiling beef /other stock
- 3 Tbs olive oil
- 2 mature Williams pears
- 200 g sweet gorgonzola
- 4 Tbs grated parmesan
- 1 cup 'Vin Santo' sweet wine
- salt

Thinly slice the scallions and sauté in the oil with 1 tbs of butter. As soon as the scallions are translucent around 5-6 minutes at this point add the peeled and thinly sliced pears and cook together for 10mins. Add the rice and pinch of salt and toast over high heat for about 2-4 minutes stirring constantly. Add the Vin Santo wine and once it evaporates begin to add in the broth a little at a time. Stir occasionally and add two pinches of salt to the mixture while it is cooking. Continue to gradually add small amounts of the boiled broth allowing each addition to be absorbed before adding the next. Stir it from time to time keeping the rice from sticking to the bottom of the pan. Use a medium heat and cook slowly uncovered. After 15-20 minutes the rice will be cooked. Remove from heat and add the remaining butter, parmesan and cubes of gorgonzola and stir through the rice well. Cover and leave to stand 2 minutes. Serve hot.

# *Risotto di zucca*

## Pumpkin risotto

Serves 4

- 320 g arborio rice
- 1 scallion
- 1 onion, chopped finely and slightly browned
- 1 glass of dry white wine
- 5 Tbs of grated parmesan cheese
- 30 g butter
- 6 Tbs olive oil
- 800 g pumpkin
- 2 L vegetable broth

In a saucepan brown the finely chopped scallion in olive oil then add the coarsely grated pumpkin. Allow to cook for 10 mins on a high flame. Lower the flame, add a good pinch of salt, cover and let cook slowly for 15 minutes. In a second saucepan brown the chopped onion in the butter, add the rice and let toast for 2 mins, stirring constantly. Add the white wine and allow it to evaporate for around 3 mins. Begin to add the vegetable broth a little at a time. Add salt to taste and when the risotto is half cooked, at around 8 mins, add the cooked pumpkin. You need to make sure that the pumpkin is kept hot until it is added. Continue to cook the rice adding the broth until the rice is almost done. Turn off the flame, add the parmesan cheese and the butter, mix well, then let sit for 3 minutes before serving. You can garnish with parmesan or chives.

# *Risotto ai porcini*

## Porcini mushroom risotto

Serves 4

- 320 g Arborio rice
- 800 g fresh porcini mushrooms
- 2 garlic cloves
- parsley or 'nepitella' – this is a typical herb that is used in italy when cooking mushrooms
- salt and pepper
- olive oil

Remove the stalks of the mushrooms and clean the cap and the stalk with a knife. Cut the cap and the stalk into medium sized pieces.
In a saucepan, sautè the garlic and the herb in 5 tablespoons of oil, before the garlic becomes golden brown add the mushrooms and salt and pepper then cook slowly with the cover for 15 minutes. Using the basic risotto recipe, add the mushrooms 5 minutes before the rice is cooked.

This mushroom recipe can also be used to dress home made pasta, for crostoni (toasted bread), with polenta with a sprinkle of parmesan.

# *Risotto di Carciofi*

## Artichoke risotto

**For the Artichokes: refer to the recipe on page, 124.**

**For risotto: follow the recipe for 'Basic Risotto' on page 66.**

# *Risotto 'Primavera'*

## Spring risotto

Serves 4

- 320 g Arborio rice
- 3 carrots
- bunch of asparagus
- fresh peas
- 3 shallots
- 1 glass of white wine
- 1.5 L vegetable broth
- 4 Tbs grated parmesan
- salt to taste
- peperoncino (add just a little bit and taste before adding more!)

Saute in 6 tbs olive oil all of the roughly chopped vegetables for about 10 mins on medium flame. Then add the rice and toast for about 2 mins in the vegetables. Add the wine and let evaporate for around 3 mins. Add a generous pinch of salt, and now it is time to start adding the broth (make sure it is boiling!). Add the broth bit by bit and the rice will take about 15 minutes to be done. Now remove from the flame, add the grated parmesan and if you like a small knob of butter to give it a creamy taste.
Lightly stir, cover and leave for 2 mins before serving.

# *Risotto all'ortica*

## Stinging nettle risotto

Serves 4

- 320 g Arborio rice
- 2 cups nettle tips (not flowered)
- extra virgin olive oil
- 1 onion
- prosecco
- vegetable stock
- butter
- salt and pepper

In a pan fry an onion in some olive oil, once it has browned add the washed and dried nettle tips. After 2 minutes we add the rice, after another 2 minutes we add a good amount of prosecco! Let the alcohol evaporate. During the cooking we continuously add some vegetable stock making sure the rice doesn't stick to the bottom of the pan. Cooking time will take about 15-20 minutes. Stir in a generous dob of butter and lots of parmesan cheese. Let sit for 4 minutes before serving.

# *Risotto con scamorza e spumante*

## Champagne and scamorza cheese risotto

Serves 4

- 320 g Arborio rice
- 150 g smoked scamorza cheese
- 1 bottle of Brut Spumante
- ½ L of salted vegetable broth (you can also add salt if necessary)
- extra virgin olive oil

Heat a few tablespoons of oil in a deep frypan (better to use a frypan rather than a saucepan as the rice has more coverage on the heated pan therefore allowing it to cook better). Once the oil has heated for a couple of minutes, add the rice. Let it toast for around 3-5 mins, then add the entire bottle of champagne. Bring to the boil, continuously stirring for around 10 mins or until the rice starts to thicken and the liquid evapo-

rates. In the last 5 mins add the vegetable broth and the smoked scamorza cheese. Make sure to stir continuously with a wooden spoon. Take off the heat before the rice becomes too soft. Let sit for a few minutes, covered. This allows the risotto to become a little thicker and creamier.

# *Risotto alla Toscana*

## Traditional Tuscan risotto

Serves 4

- 320 g Arborio rice
- 70 g butter
- 50 g minced meat
- the meat of 1 chicken
- 100 g chicken livers
- 1 glass dry white wine
- extra virgin olive oil
- 1 can of tinned tomatoes
- 1 onion
- 1 carrot
- a celery stick
- 1 L of beef, veal or chicken broth
- 4 Tbs grated parmesan

Prepare the chicken, removing the meat from the bones. Finely chop the carrot, half an onion, the celery and sautè in 2 tbs olive oil and 40 g butter. Add the mince, the roughly chopped chicken and chopped livers. After a minute or so add the wine and let evaporate on a high heat for another couple of minutes. Add the tinned tomatoes, salt and pepper. When the chicken is well cooked remove from the saucepan and keep it aside to use for a main meal. In another saucepan add the other half of the chopped onion, the butter and the rice and let toast for a few minutes on a relatively high heat though making sure to not let the butter burn. Add a ladle full of the boiling broth and cook the rice until about two thirds done, mixing and adding broth as you need it. Add half of the meat mix to the rice and finish the cooking. When the rice is ready you will serve it with an extra spoonful of the broth on top and abundent parmesan cheese.

# *Crespelle alla Fiorentina*

## Florentine spinach and ricotta crepes

Serves 6

**For the batter:**

- 150 g flour
- 3 eggs
- 300 ml milk
- 75 g melted butter
- salt

Mix the flour, egg, melted butter and salt. Then add lukewarm milk, mix thoroughly and let it rest for at least 30 minutes.

**For the bechamel sauce:**

- 1 L milk
- 100 g butter
- 80 g flour

Melt the butter in a saucepan. Add flour, then cook for a minute. Next add the milk, mixing constantly. Bring it to simmering point and cook it until the sauce becomes thick. Add salt and nutmeg to taste and then set it aside.

**For the tomato sauce:**

- 400 g tomatoes, peeled and diced
- 1 garlic clove, peeled and crushed

For the tomato sauce, sautè the garlic in a tablespoon of oil, and add the chopped tomatoes. Cook for 5 minutes then add a couple of basil leaves. Set aside.

**For the filling:**

- 800 g spinach with the thick part of the stalk removed
- 300 g ricotta
- 3 Tbs grated parmesan
- 1 egg
- 1 pinch nutmeg
- salt and black pepper to taste

Wash the spinach twice and cook it using just the water left on the leaves from the rinsing. Squeeze it well, then chop finely. Mix the ricotta with the cooled-down spinach, salt, pepper, nutmeg, egg and parmesan cheese and put it in the fridge.

**To prepare and serve the crepes:**
Using a small ladle, spoon the batter into a small, non-stick frypan and tip the pan to spread the batter around evenly. This amount of batter should make 12 crepes. Fill each crepe with a heaped tablespoon of the ricotta and spinach mixture then fold the crepes over and put them onto a greased oven tray. Cover the crepes with bechamel, parmesan cheese and garnish with the tomato sauce. Grill them in the oven until they are lightly browned.

## *Crespelle ai funghi porcini e tartufo*

### Crepes with porcini mushrooms and truffle

Serves 10

**For the crepes: refer to recipe on page 74**
**Bechamel sauce: refer to recipe on page 74**
**Porcini mushroom filling: refer to recipe on page 10**

- Fresh truffle (white is the best), or truffle cream.

Fill each crepe with the chopped mushrooms and bechamel sauce mixed in. Fold in half, and cook in the microwave for one minute. Top with bechamel sauce that has been combined with some truffle cream. Shave a bit of fresh truffle on top of each crepe before serving.

# *Pasta e ceci*

## Pasta and garbanzo bean soup

Serves 4

- 300 g dried garbanzo beans (chickpeas)
- 1 tsp baking soda/bicarbonate of soda
- 4 cloves garlic, bruised
- 2 sprigs rosemary
- 6 Tbs extra virgin olive oil
- 2 Tbs tomato concentrate/purée
- salt and freshly ground black pepper
- 250-500 ml stock (homemade or bouillon cube)
- 200 g tagliatelle pasta, broken into short lengths (you can also use the small short and stubby 'rigatoni' pasta)

In Tuscany this dish is traditionally cooked in a deep, flameproof earthenware dish.

Rinse the beans well and place in a large bowl of cold water with the baking soda. Leave to soak overnight or for at least 12 hours. Drain, transfer to a colander and rinse thoroughly under cold running water. Place in a saucepan and cover with cold water. Add 2 garlic cloves and a sprig of rosemary. Cover, leaving space for steam to escape and simmer for about 1 hour, or until the beans are very tender, adding a pinch of salt after about 50 minutes. Drain and keep the cooking water to use later. Purée three- quarters of the garbanzo beans in a food processor or food mill, keeping the remainder whole. Heat half the olive oil in a large heavy-bottomed saucepan and sauté the remaining garlic and rosemary sprig for 3 minutes. Add the tomato purée and continue cooking over a moderate heat for 2 minutes. Add the puréed and whole garbanzo beans and the reserved cooking liquid and bring to a boil. If the soup is very thick, dilute with a little hot stock. Add the tagliatelle (or other pasta) and cook for about 10 mins until the pasta is ready. Remember, if you are using fresh pasta you will only need about 3-4 minutes until the pasta will be ready. If you have made a large quantity of soup, add the pasta only to the quantity of soup you would like to eat. Reheating the soup with the pasta the next day is not the best way to serve it. It is always best to add new pasta each time you eat the soup. Season with salt and pepper and a generous dash of extra virgin olive oil.

# *Salse e sughi*

## Salsas and sauces

# *Pesto*

## Basil and pinenut sauce

Serves 4

- 4 bunches of fresh basil
- 1 clove of garlic
- 4 Tbs of parmesan cheese
- 1 Tbs of pecorino cheese
- 2 Tbs pine nuts
- 1 cup of olive oil
- 2 pinches salt
- 1 pinch of white pepper

Remove the basil leaves from the stems and put in the blender together with the other ingredients leaving the oil until the end. Mix on low speed for 3 seconds. Put the pesto in a bowl and stir with a wooden spoon. Add more salt and pepper to taste.

# *Pumarola*

## Tomato and basil sauce

Serves 4

- 1.5 kg of fresh very mature tomatoes or 1 can crushed tomato
- 3 gloves of garlic
- bunch of fresh basil
- olive oil
- salt and pepper

*If you like a spicier sauce add some fresh peperoncino (chili) with the garlic but garnish with parsley.*

Crush the garlic with the back of a knife. In a saucepan heat 8 tbs of oil, add the garlic, basil (if NOT using chili), and heat for 2 minutes. Then add the tomatoes, a pinch of salt and pepper. Let simmer for 10 minutes for canned tomatoes, or if using fresh tomoates then wash and cut them into small pieces add them to the oil and let reduce before passing the mixture through a food mill, until there is nothing remaining bar the skins. Put the sauce back on the stove and simmer until it becomes thick.
When adding to pasta (both fresh and dry), bring a large saucepan of water to boil and then add a handful of rock salt. Once the water has reached a 'rolling boil' again you can now add the pasta.
When cooked 'al dente' (this is important as the pasta will continue to cook with the sauce, if the packet says to cook for 8 mins then remove 2 mins before for spaghetti) take out of the water with a large strainer and add to the sauce. Sautè together on a live flame for 2 minutes then serve. Add grated parmesan, a drizzle of good extra virgin olive oil and also fresh basil leaves to garnish (or parsley if chili has been used).

# *Ragù di carne* #1

## Meat ragù # 1

Serves 6

- 1 red onion
- 1 stick of celery
- 3 carrots
- 300 g of minced beef or veal
- 1 sausage (optional)
- 500 g peeled mature tomatoes
- ground pepper
- 1 glass of red wine

Finely dice the first three ingredients and place into a pan with plenty of oil and cook for about 15 minutes or until softened, on a low to medium flame, being careful that the vegetables do not stick to the pan. Stir often, and begin adding the meat and sausage with the vegetables. Continue cooking the mixture another 15-20 minutes or until the meat has browned. At this time, add the wine and allow it to evaporate well. Pass the tomatoes through a food mill then add to the mixture. Add salt and pepper to taste. Cook at a low heat for about 1½ hours more, stirring from time to time as it tends to stick.

# *Ragù di carne* #2

## Meat ragù # 2

Serves 6

- 1 onion, chopped finely
- 1 carrot, chopped finely
- 1 celery stalk, chopped finely
- 5 parsley stalks, chopped finely
- 100 ml extra virgin olive oil
- 400 g minced beef
- 1 pork sausage, skinned and chopped
- 1 glass dry red wine
- 400 g tomatoes, peeled and chopped
- 2 ladles meat stock
- 1 tsp salt
- Optional: 25 g dried porcini mushrooms, soaked and chopped

Sautè the vegetables in the oil until lightly golden. Add the mince and the sausage. Cook and stir until browned. Add the wine and stir until it evaporates. Add the tomatoes, stock and salt. Let it simmer for a couple of hours. If it dries out, add a little stock or water. At the end of the cooking process, add salt to taste.

# *Sugo all'anatra*

## Duck ragù

Serves 6

- ½ a full size duck, including the liver and heart
- 50 g pancetta (not smoked)
- 450 g canned tomotoes
- 1 medium red onion
- 1 carrots
- 1 celery stalks
- 1 glass of red wine
- salt and pepper
- 4 tbs olive oil

Sautè the finely chopped carrot, onion, celery and chopped pancetta in 4 tablespoons of olive oil for 10-15 minutes until the mixture is quite reduced, being careful not to burn it. Add the heart and liver of the duck. Cut the duck into 3 smaller pieces so they fit into the pan and add. Cook all together for about 10 minutes, allowing the meat of the duck to break off and the heart and liver to also break apart. Add the red wine. When the wine evaporates, blend the tomatoes in a mixer and then add to the saucepan with the duck. Add salt and pepper to taste and cook on a low flame for about 1 hour. Remove the bones from the saucepan. You will need to pull off all of the meat remaining, chop finely and add back into the saucepan. Cook for another 10-15 minutes.
This is commonly served in Tuscany with 'pappardelle' or 'tagliatelle' pasta. You could also use this to top polenta.

**Alternative:** *The same recipe can be substituted with rabbit, hare or pheasant.*

# *Salsa di noci e gorgonzola*

## Gorgonzola and walnut sauce

Serves 4

- 200 g gorgonzola cheese
- 8 walnuts
- 125 g of liquid cream
- 4 Tbs grated parmesan

Crush nuts finely in a mixer. Place in a mixing bowl, add all other ingredients and mix well with a wooden spoon. **Do not cook this mixture.**

This can be used for both crostini and also as a sauce for pasta.
For pasta, cook the pasta as normal. When the pasta is cooked, drain and then add the sauce and toss well. Save a little water that you have used to cook the pasta and this can be used to thin the sauce if needed.

# *Sugo ai funghi*

## Mushroom sauce

- 250 g dried mushrooms
- 2 cloves of garlic
- olive oil
- nipitella herbs
- 1 Tbs of butter
- ½ L of beef broth

In a bowl of luke warm water add the mushrooms and let sit for 30 minutes. In a sauce pan put ½ cup olive oil, pressed garlic and sauté. Take the mushrooms from the water, remove the excess water, chop and add to saucepan. Cook over a low flame for about 3 minutes. Add the nipitella that has been chopped finely. Now add the broth and cook slowly over a low flame for 20 minutes stirring occassionally, adding more broth as necessary. Remove from the flame and stir in the butter, cover and let

it rest for another 30 minutes. This mixture can also be used to top polenta for a delicious first course or as a 'crostini' on top of toasted Italian bread.

## *Salsa Besciamella*

### Bechamel sauce

Makes 3 cups
A fundamental ingredient used in many lasagna, cannelloni and sformato recipes.

- 3 cups of milk
- 5 Tbs plain flour
- 5 Tbs butter
- white pepper
- nutmeg (optional)
- salt

In a saucepan (heavy bottomed) melt the butter then add the flour and cook for a few minutes at a moderate heat, whisking briskly and continuously until the flour and butter are mixed well. Heat the milk separately then once milk boils remove from heat and slowly add the boiled milk a little at a time stirring continually, keeping the mixture smooth. Add salt and pepper to taste and a pinch of nutmeg and cook at low heat for about 10-12 minutes until the mixture thickens.

It is best is the mixture is used immediately but it can be covered and stored for up to 2 hours though you must reheat before using.

# *Sugo finto*
## Meatless Ragu

Serves 4
- 2 carrots
- 2 onions
- 2 celery stalks
- 1 garlic clove
- 2 sage leaves
- 1 twig rosemary
- 1 tablespoon of tomato concentrate
- 8 tablespoons of extra virgin olive oil
- 1 glass of red wine
- 20 gr dried porcini mushrooms
- 500 mls of vegetable broth

Place the dried mushrooms to regenerate in cold water.
Finely chop the vegetables and herbs together. You can use the food processor for this if you like.
Place the broth to boil, remove the mushrooms from the water, squeeze out any excess and chop finely. Keep the water from the soaked mushrooms.
Place the vegetables and herbs in the frypan with the oil and when golden wet with the red wine, let evaporate and then add the tomato concentrate.
Wet with boiling broth , add the mushrooms and also the water used to soak them . Pay attention that there is no dirt remaining trom the mushrooms.
Let cook on a low flame for 40 mins.
Fantastic with fresh tagliatelle or with potato ravioli or tortelli.

# *Sugo di coniglio*

## Rabbit sauce Chianti Style

Serves 6-8

- An entire rabbit of approximately 1 kilo
- 400g canned tomatoes
- 3 garlic cloves
- 200g onion
- 100g celery
- 100g carrot
- 3 bay leaves
- 200ml Chianti wine
- 200ml extra virgin olive oil
- salt & pepper to taste

Preparation Time - 30 mins
Cooking Time - 2 hours

Prepare a 'battuto' with the carrot, celery & onion ( this mean chop them all finely together) and put them in a pan with the olive oil and the bay leaves to start to soften and brown. Let cook on a medium heat for about 20 mins taking care to not let them burn, then add the rabbit that has been cut up into pieces and let brown. Wet with the Chianti wine. At this point you need to wash and divide the rabbits head into two pieces and place it in another pan with olive oil on a high heat for a couple of minute to brown. After all of the rabbit pieces have browned, you need to remove the bones, and finely chop the remaining meat. Some people at this point pass everything through a food mill , the hand operated one being better as an electrical mill may liquidize it which you don't want!
Return to the saucepan on a low to medium and add the tinned tomatoes and let everything cook together. In Tuscany when it wasn't possible to prepare the 'sugo al lepre' which means 'Hare Sauce', often when the hunters weren't skilled enough to catch their prey, the rabbit would substitute as the 'poor' cousin. If it bothers you to use the head of the rabbit, this can be left out though 'i buongustai' ( the people that know their food!) say they can notice a significant difference in the resulting sauce.
It is better to use fresh pasta with this sauce.

# *Secondi Piatti*

## Mains

# *Pollo all'Etrusca*

## Etruscan chicken

Serves 4

- 1 Tbs vinegar
- 1 chicken
- 100 g black olives
- 1 red onion
- rosemary and sage
- 1 cup of white wine
- pinenuts
- raisins/sultanas
- salt and pepper

Cut the chicken into 12 pieces and leave to sit in a bowl with cold water and 1 tablespoon of vinegar. In a casserole dish put 6 tablespoons of olive oil and finely chopped onion and sautè for about 10 minutes, then add the chicken without the water and sautè together. When the chicken is browned salt and pepper to taste, add the white wine and cook slowly for about 20 minutes in a covered casserole dish. Add the pinenuts and the raisins, stir, recover and let cook for a further 10 minutes.
Before removing from the heat, add the olives, sage and rosemary finely chopped.
Let set for 15 minutes and serve!

# *Pollo ripieno con pistacchi, salsiccia e prosciutto*

## Chicken stuffed with crushed pistaccio, pork and ham

Serves 4

- 1 whole chicken deboned
- 5 slices of fontina cheese
- 5 slices of proscuitto cotto
- 3 Tbs of crushed pistaccio nuts
- 150 g ground pork mince
- salt and pepper to taste
- chopped sage and rosemary
- ½ glass white wine
- 6 Tbs olive oil

Preheat the oven to 180°C. Mix the chopped herbs in with the pork mince. The chicken, after the butcher has deboned it, will be relatively flat with two holes, one on each end.
Layer the cheese, ham, crushed nuts and then the mince inside the chicken. This needs to then be rolled, making sure that the holes of the chicken are closed inside the roll. You will then need to tie securely with baking string. Place in a baking dish, cover wth 6 tablespoons of extra virgin olive oil. Place in the oven and after 15 minutes, wet with half a glass of dry white wine. Return to the oven for another hour.

**Alternative:** *you can also use chicken or turkey breasts for this recipe, they may be less fiddly. You can also vary what you stuff the meat with. Artichokes in season are great or also asparagus. Chestnuts in autumn also pair nicely with the chicken.*

# *Involtini di pollo ripieni con carciofi e fontina*

## Chicken rolls stuffed with artichoke and fontina cheese

Serves 4

- 4 chicken breasts
- 4 artichokes
- 1 lemon
- 1 bunch of parsley
- 1 bunch of sage
- 3 garlic clove
- 4 slices of fontina cheese
- 4 slices of pancetta or bacon

Squeeze the juice of one lemon into a bowl filled with cold water.
Clean the artichokes (cut half of the stalk off, about 2-3 cms from the tip of the artichoke and remove the external leaves - the hard ones).
Immediately brush with the lemon to prevent the artichokes from turning black when exposed to the air. Cut the artichokes in half and then cut in thin slices, place them in the bowl with the lemon water.
Take a saucepan and add the olive oil, the pressed cloves of garlic and parsley. When the oil is hot remove the artichokes from the water and cook for 5 minutes on a hot flame, stirring continually.
Lower the flame, add salt and pepper, cover and cook for about 10-15 mins. Pay attention as if the steam is not sufficient to cook the artichokes (this will depend on the quality and freshness of the artichokes and the strength of the gas), add same hot water, a little at a time.
You will know when they are cooked when they are soft but not falling apart.
Chicken breasts are normally quite thick, you or your butcher can cut them in half again to have thinner more workable pieces.
Take a piece of chicken breast, add a slice of fontina cheese then some cooked artichoke and close with a toothpick. Roll the piece of pancetta around the outside of the chicken roll, add an entire sage leaf and if necessary close wth a piece of cooking string.
To cook - In a saucepan heat 6 tablespoons of olive oil with the garlic clo-

ves and cook the chicken rolls for 3-4 minutes, turning constantly until they are a dark golden brown. Add salt, pepper and ½ cup of white wine, lower the flame, cover and cook for another 10 minutes. Wet with more wine if you feel it needs it.

When artichokes are not in season you can substitute with asparagus or even make an omelette with egg and spinach and wrap that up inside the chicken.

## *Faraona arrosto con uva e mele*

### Baked guinea fowl marinated with grapes, apple and white wine

Serves 4

- 1 Guinea Fowl
- 15 white grapes (seedless)
- 1 granny smith apple
- 6 thin slices of pancetta (not smoked)
- sage
- rosemary
- salt and pepper
- olive oil
- 1 glass white wine

Clean guinea fowl and remove heart, blood, liver, etc.
Cut the grapes in half, cut the apples (leaving the skin) into quarters and rub generously with salt and pepper.
Stuff the fowl with the fruit. Under the wings place 3 leaves of sage and a twig of rosemary. Place the slices of pancetta over the breast of the fowl. With kitchen string wrap the fowl, making sure that the wings and legs are pulled close to the body of the bird. The bottom of the fowl will need to be closed with a couple of toothpicks to ensure that the grapes don't come out.
Place the fowl in a baking dish, sprinkle with a little salt and pepper, drizzle with olive oil and bake in a 180°C oven for 45 minutes. Remove from oven, remove the pancetta and the string from the bird, though place the pancetta in the baking dish to continue flavouring the sauces and place in the oven again for about 15 minutes.

Remove from oven and remove toothpicks. Lift the bird slightly allowing the fruit to come out, along with the juices into the baking dish. The fowl will then be removed and placed into the serving dish. The fruit and juice and pancetta will need to be filtered with a sieve into a small saucepan. Add the white wine and cook together on a medium flame for 10 minutes. This is then used as the gravy to serve with the guinea fowl.

***Alternative:*** *You can also substitute the guinea fowl with chicken, pheasant or even pork is nice served with the fruit and white wine.*

# *Pollo in Fricassea*

## Chicken Fricassee

Serves 6

- 1 large chicken
- 60gr of 'lard' which is thinly sliced cured pigs fat juice of 2 lemons
- 1 glass of meat broth
- 1 small bunch chopped parsley
- ½ stick of cinnamon
- ½ onion with 3 cloves
- 1 egg yolk

Cut the chicken into 12 pieces. Take a saucepan, add the chopped lard and allow the chicken to brown in the fat. Remove the chicken, discard the fat that remains on the bottom. Add the chopped parsley, the juice of ½ lemon , the cinnamon stick and the onion (with the cloves stuck in it). Add two small pinches of salt and wet with the boiling broth, cover and let cook for 30 minutes at a low flame. After this remove the chicken pieces from the pan and let the sauce reduce further 3-4 minutes. Remove the onion and the cinnamon, beat the egg yolk adding the remainder of the lemon juice and add to the saucepan. As soon as the sauce starts to bubble again add the chicken pieces , turning them to allow the sauce to evenly cover, add the chopped parsley and serve hot.

**NOTE :** Any meat can be substituted, lamb, rabbit and veal are commonly substituted.

# *Faraona alla cacciatora con funghi*

## Guinea fowl with mushrooms... Hunter Style

Serves 4

- 1 whole Guinea Fowl cut into 8 pieces
- 35 g dried porcini mushrooms
- 30 g butter
- 8 Tbs olive oil
- 1 small onion
- 3 cloves garlic
- ½ glass dry white wine
- 350 g chopped tinned tomatoes
- parsley
- 1 Tbs flour
- salt and pepper

Place the mushrooms in a bowl with warm water for one hour to re-hydrate. In a saucepan heat the oil and add the chopped onions and the squashed garlic (not crushed but squashed with the back of a knife). Allow to cook for around 10 minutes then add the guinea fowl. Let the fowl brown on all sides, then add the wine and let evaporate for 3 minutes. Add the flour and mix well with the guinea fowl pieces, covering totally. You can then add the tomatoes, flavour with salt and pepper and let cook, covered on a low flame for around 30 minutes.
In a second saucepan heat the butter with a garlic clove and then add the drained mushrooms and let cook for around 30 minutes, finishing with the chopped parsley.
At this point the bird will also be almost cooked, so add the mushrooms and let the flavours unite for 10 minutes on a low flame.
Turn off the stove and let sit covered for 15 minutes, then serve.

**Alternative:** *You can also substitute the guinea fowl with chicken, rabbit or even turkey.*

# *Coniglio al Chianti*

## Rabbit cooked with Chianti

Serves 3-4

- 1 rabbit
- 750 ml Chianti wine
- 100 ml wine vinegar
- ½ onion chopped
- 1 stalk of chopped celery
- 1 chopped carrot
- thyme
- 4 cloves of garlic
- 200 g peeled tomatoes
- pinch of salt and pepper
- stock
- 100 ml olive oil
- 30 g flour

Cut the rabbit into pieces. Prepare the marinade with the wine, vinegar, onion, celery, carrot and thyme. Leave to marinate for around 12 hours. Remove the rabbit pieces from the marinade, pat dry with kitchen towel and cover well with the flour. In a pan heat the olive oil and add the garlic and the thyme used for marinating, when it has turned brown add the rabbit pieces. Once the meat has a good colour add the remaining marinade and the tomatoes. Cook on a medium heat and if necessary add a bit of stock. Salt and pepper to taste.

**Alternative:** *You can also substitute the rabbit with chicken.*

# *Cinghiale in umido*

## Wild boar stew

Serves 4

- 800 g wild boar meat
- 50 g pancetta ham
- 500 g  chopped tomatoes
- 2 garlic cloves
- 3 glasses of red wine
- 2 tsp fennel seeds
- 3 bay leaves
- 2 balls of ginepro (juniper)
- ½ glass of red wine vinegar
- salt and pepper
- 8 Tbs olive oil

Cut the wild boar meat into small pieces and place in a dish with 1 teaspoon of crushed fennel seeds, 2 glasses of red wine, ½ glass of vinegar, salt and pepper. Cover and leave to marinate all night in the fridge.

**The day after:** Slightly brown the pancetta ham in a heavy bottomed saucepan with oil, the bay leaves and the juniper, then add the wild boar meat and let brown over a medium flame for 5 or 6 minutes, adding 1 glass of red wine. When this has evaporated add 1 tsp of crushed fennel seeds and salt and pepper.

Let cook for another 5 minutes, then add the tomatoes and let cook on a very low flame for about 2 hours.

*This is fantastic served on a bed of polenta or also as a 'sugo' (sauce) on pasta, especially 'pappardelle' which are the flat ribbon like egg pasta commonly enjoyed in Tuscany. The wild boar can also be served with rosemary potatoes.*

# *Ossobuco*

## Tuscan braised veal shanks

Serves 4

- 4 veal shanks cut to around 3 cms thick
- 1 onion
- 1 stalk of celery
- 1 carrot
- 20 g butter
- olive oil
- 1 tin of peeled tomatoes
- 1 Tbs flour

*'Ossobuco'* when translated means *'bone'* and *'hole'* and it is the bone-marrow inside of the veal shank that helps give this dish such a wonderful flavour.

Make a 'battuto' with the onion, celery and carrot. This means simply to finely chop everything.
In a saucepan unite 4 tbs olive oil and 20 g butter. Add the vegetables and cook on a low flame for 10 minutes. Lightly cover the ossobuco with the flour and then add to the saucepan.
Add salt and pepper, the tinned tomatoes (first blend in a food processor) and cook, covered for about 1 ½ hours on a low flame.
The sauce that you have at the end is optimal for topping a rice pilaf, pasta or baked potatoes to accompany the ossobuco.

# *Polpette di ricotta e vitella*

## Veal and ricotta meat balls

Serves 8

**For the meat balls:**

- 500 g veal mince (finely minced)
- 400 g sheep ricotta cheese
- 2 eggs
- 150 g parmesan cheese
- a pinch of nutmeg
- a pinch of salt
- a pinch of black pepper
- oil for frying (sunflower or peanut oil)

Using your hands, mix all the ingredients together until you obtain a smooth mixture. Form rissoles about the size of an egg and flour them. In a deep frypan, fry a few meat balls at a time in the hot oil turning them in the oil. Drain them on kitchen paper.

**For the sauce:**

- 3 garlic cloves, crushed
- 4 Tbs extra virgin olive oil
- 800 g diced, peeled tomatoes
- a pinch of salt
- 6 basil leaves

Sautè the garlic in a saucepan. Add the tomatoes and salt and cook for 10 minutes. Then add the meat balls and basil leaves. Cook for another 5 minutes and serve, garnishing with extra basil leaves.

# *Lesso in francesina*

## Boiled beef with onions

Serves 4

**For the *Francesina* sauce:**

- 1 kg onion, thinly sliced
- 1 carrot, finely chopped
- 1 celery stalk
- 4 tomatoes, diced

In a saucepan sautè the onions, carrot and celery. Add the tomatoes. Salt and pepper to taste and cook for 15 min.

**For the boiled meat:**

- 800 g beef
- 1 carrot
- 1 onion
- 1 celery stalk

Simmer the meat for 2 - 3 hours. When the meat is ready, dice it and place it in the saucepan with the *Francesina* sauce. Cover with stock and simmer gently for a further 20 minutes until the stock is reduced. Any leftovers can also be served on hot toasted bread or used as a pasta sauce.

# *Involtini di vitella al latte*

## Veal rolls cooked in milk

Serves 4

- 8 slices of veal
- 4 thick slices of ham
- 500 g spinach with the thick part of the stalk removed
- 400 ml milk
- 20 g unsalted butter
- 20 g olive oil
- fresh sage and rosemary
- flour
- 2 garlic cloves
- a pinch of nutmeg

Wash the spinach, put it in a pot with the lid on and cook it gently until it loses its volume. Let it cool then chop it. Flatten the veal with a meat mallet then salt it and add half a slice of ham and the spinach. Roll the veal slices and secure with a toothpick or kitchen string. Toss in flour. In a pan, heat the butter with the crushed cloves of garlic then brown the rolls of veal and add the hot milk and nutmeg. When the milk starts to boil, cover and cook for about 30 minutes. When cooked, take the toothpicks out and put the rolls on a serving dish. Then pass the sauce through a fine strainer o in a blender and pour it on the rolls. Serve immediately.

# Polpettone di carne alla Fiorentina

## Florentine meat loaf

Serves 4

- 500 g beef mince
- 100 g prosciutto, chopped finely or minced
- 2 eggs
- 1 garlic clove, chopped finely
- a handful of parsley, chopped finely
- 100 g of bread, crust removed, soaked in milk and then squeezed to remove excess liquid
- 50 g grated parmesan cheese
- bread crumbs
- olive oil
- a pinch salt
- a pinch ground black pepper
- 500 g tomatoes, peeled and diced
- 200 ml red wine
- 1 garlic clove, peeled and crushed
- 1 small onion, chopped finely
- 1 carrot, chopped finely
- 1 celery stalk, chopped finely
- 6 Tbs olive oil

Mix the mince, prosciutto, eggs, chopped garlic, parsley, grated parmesan cheese and bread in a bowl until you obtain a smooth mixture. Sautè the crushed garlic clove, onion, carrot, and celery in the olive oil. Meanwhile, roll the mixture into tubular shape, roll it through the breadcrumbs and add it to the pan to brown. Add the wine and when it has evaporated add the tomatoes, a pinch of salt and pepper. Cook on a low heat for about 1 hour. Taste for salt and pepper and adjust as necessary. Slice the *polpettone* and serve the slices covered in their sauce.

# *Salsicce e fagioli all'uccelletto*

## Tuscan pork sausages with cannellini beans

Serves 4

**To cook the beans:**

- 400 g dry cannellini beans
- 2 L cold water
- 2 garlic cloves
- 2 Tbs extra virgin olive oil
- 1 small sprig of sage
- 1 tsp salt
- a few peppercorns

Put the cannellini beans in a pot. Add the water, garlic, oil, sage, salt and pepper, cover with a lid and place over a low flame. The water must simmer gently and not boil. The beans will take 2 to 3 hours to cook.

**To finish off the dish:**

- 400 g diced, peeled tomatoes
- 4 garlic cloves, crushed
- 4 - 5 sage leaves
- 4 Tuscan-style pork sausages
- 8 tbs extra virgin olive oil
- salt and pepper

Brown the sausages in 8 tablespoons of oil then pierce them with a fork. Add the garlic and sage leaves, then add the previously cooked beans. Add salt and pepper and let them cook for a few minutes.
Then add the tomatoes. Cook gently until the sausages are cooked and the juices have reduced.

# *Arista alla Fiorentina*

## Florentine roasted pork loin

Serves 6

- 1.5 kg pork loin, with the bone
- 2 garlic cloves, chopped finely
- the leaves of 2 sprigs of rosemary, chopped finely
- 2 pinches of salt
- 2 pinches of ground black pepper
- 200 ml extra virgin olive oil

Ask your butcher to de-bone the loin and to give you the bone.
Mix garlic, rosemary, salt and pepper. Put ½ of this mixture between the loin and the bone then tie the bone and loin together and rub in the rest of the mixture, evenly covering all the meat.
Put the loin in a baking dish, pour over the oil and cook in a 175 °C oven for about an hour and a half, basting the meat every now and then with the cooking juices.
Once cooked, cover with aluminium foil and let it rest for 10 minutes. Untie the meat, remove the bone and slice thinly. Serve with the cooking juices.

# *Arista marinata con l'uva*

## Baked pork with grapes

Serves 6

- 1 kg piece of pork loin
- 2 twigs rosemary
- 10 sage leaves
- 40 grapes (red or green or a mix)
- 1 tsp salt
- fresh black pepper
- ½ cup extra virgin olive oil
- 1 glass of white wine

Preheat oven to 250°C. Chop the rosemary and sage finely, mix well with fresh black pepper and a teaspoon of salt. Rub the pork loin all over with this mixture, then place in a baking dish, drizzling the meat with half a cup of olive oil. Place the meat in the pre-heated oven for 20 minutes. While the meat is in the oven, cut the grapes in half and remove the seeds. Mix the grapes with a little olive oil, salt and pepper and let marinate for 20 minutes.
After 20 minutes remove the pork and turn the heat down to 160°C. Add the white wine and the grapes to the pork and return to the oven for 40 minutes occasionally basting the pork with the juices.

# *Arista arrosto con scalogni e finocchio*

## Baked pork with spring onions and fennel

Serves 4

- 1 loin of pork (about 600 g)
- juice of 1 orange
- fresh sage and rosemary
- 6 fennel
- 6 scallions

- salt and pepper
- 1 glass of white wine
- ½ cup olive oil

Preheat oven to 200°C. Finely chop the rosemary and sage and rub, along with the salt and pepper, all over the pork loin. Place the pork in oven with some olive oil. Allow 30 minutes at 200 °C to brown on both sides.
Cook the scallions and fennel with oil. When browned, after 10 minutes, turn off the heat. Remove the pork, squeeze an orange and pour the wine over the meat. Place the scallions and fennel evenly around the pork in the pan and then place again in oven for 1 hour at 150°C.
You can also substitute the fennel with carrots if you wish.

## *Peposo*

### Traditional peppery beef stew

Serves 6

- 1.2 kg boned beef shank
- 12 garlic cloves
- 1 ½ glass red wine
- 1 Tbs tomato paste
- 1/2 Tbs ground black pepper
- salt

Dice the meat. Put it in a baking dish with the garlic, wine, salt, tomato paste dissolved in some water and black pepper. Add boiling water to cover the meat and put in a 175 °C oven. Cook slowly, mixing every now and then for 2 to 3 hours until the meat is tender. If necessary, add more hot water during the cooking process. Serve the meat and sauce on toasted bread.

# *Cinghiale in dolceforte*

## Sweet and sour wild boar

Serves 6

- 1 kg wild boar from the back leg or the shoulder, diced
- 1 onion, chopped finely
- 1 carrot, chopped finely
- 1 celery stalk, chopped finely
- flour
- 1 bay leaf
- 50 g dark chocolate, grated
- 2 Tbs pine nuts
- 2 Tbs raisins, soaked in warm water
- 3 prunes, chopped
- a pinch of nutmeg
- 2 cloves
- 1 tsp sugar
- vinegar
- red wine
- meat stock
- olive oil
- salt and pepper

Marinate the wild boar in a glass of dry red wine and 3 tablespoons of vinegar overnight. Sautè the onion, carrot and celery in 8 tablespoons of oil. Dry the wild boar, flour it and add it to the pan with salt and pepper. Brown it. Add a glass of red wine, let it evaporate and add enough boiling stock to cover the meat. Simmer gently until the meat is soft.
For the sauce, mix together the chocolate, pine nuts, raisins, prunes, bay leaf, nutmeg, cloves, sugar, and ½ a glass of vinegar and set aside. When the meat is ready add the sauce, simmer for a further 5 minutes and serve.

# *Agnello alla cacciatora*

## Hunter-style lamb stew

Serves 4

- 800 g boned lamb shoulder, cut into pieces
- 400 g peeled diced tomatoes
- 1 onion, chopped finely
- 2 garlic cloves, chopped finely
- the leaves of 2 sprigs of rosemary, chopped finely
- (optional) 40 g dried porcini mushrooms, soaked in warm water and chopped finely
- 8 black olives, pitted
- 200 ml dry red wine
- 8 Tbs olive oil
- 2 pinches salt
- 1 pinch ground black pepper

Sautè the onion, garlic and rosemary with the olive oil. Then add the lamb pieces and brown for a few minutes. Add the wine and let it evaporate. Then add the tomatoes, salt and pepper and cook for about an hour and a half until the meat is soft, adding hot water if necessary. Add the porcini mushrooms and black olives 15 minutes before removing from the heat.

# *Coniglio fritto*

## Deep-fried rabbit

Serves 6

- 1 kg whole rabbit
- 2 garlic cloves, sliced
- the leaves of 2 sprigs of rosemary
- a pinch of ground black pepper
- a pinch of salt
- 250 ml dry white wine
- 50 ml extra virgin olive oil
- flour
- 3 eggs, beaten
- olive oil for frying

Make a marinade with the garlic, rosemary, pepper, salt, olive oil and wine. Cut the rabbit into small pieces and place these in the marinade for at least a couple of hours, stirring every now and then. Drain the rabbit pieces, flour them, put them in a bowl with the eggs, stir and leave them in there for an hour. Fry them in plenty of oil until golden. Drain them on kitchen paper and sprinkle with salt. Serve immediately.

**Alternative:** *You can also substitute the rabbit pieces with chicken.*

# *Anatra all'arancia*

## Orange duck

This dish originated in Tuscany during the era of Caterina de Medici, the princess who took this recipe with her when she left Italy in order to marry the future King of France, Henri II.

Serves 4

- 1.2 kg duck
- 1 orange plus the juice and zest of 3 oranges
- 2 garlic cloves
- a sprig of sage
- salt and ground black pepper
- 2 Tbs extra virgin olive oil
- 120 ml dry white wine
- 70 g butter
- 1 tsp flour
- 1 Tbs white vinegar

Burn off any bits of feathers on the duck over a gas jet flame. Empty the duck and take out the glands on the tail. Cut the wing tips, the head and the legs. Wash and dry the duck.
Stuff the duck with garlic, sage, salt and pepper and 1 whole orange. Tie the duck and place it on a baking dish, add the oil and put it in a 220° C oven. After 15 minutes add the wine and lower the temperature to 175 °C. Cook for a further 45 minutes, basting with the cooking juices every now and then.
When the duck is almost done, melt the butter in a saucepan, add the flour then add the orange juice, the zest, the vinegar, and a pinch of salt and pepper. Pour this sauce on the duck and cook for a further 10 minutes. Serve immediately.

# *Scottiglia*

This stew was one of the most popular dishes cooked by the Etruscans, and remained among the typical dishes of the Maremma area of Tuscany.

Serves 6 - 8
- 1 onion
- 5 sage leaves
- 1 bay leaf
- a piece of lemon rind
- peperoncino
- A mix of different meats cut into cubes of 3cm chicken, lamb, pork, beef, rabbit, pheasant)
- 500 gr tinned tomatoes

1 glass of white wine
- Extra Virgin olive oil
- Stale tuscan bread cut into thick slices
- Salt
- Meat Broth

**Preparation and cooking time: 2 hours**
Salt and pepper all of the pieces of meat.
In a large casserole dish pour a generous amount of olive oil and add the finely chopped onion, sage leaves and peperoncino and allow to soften on a low to medium heat. Add the pieces of meat to the casserole dish placing the pork in first, then the beef, the rabbit, lamb and chicken last as this takes the least amount of time to cook. Brown well then wet with some white wine and allow to evaporate. Add the lemon rind and allow to cook on a slow heat, adding a little hot water if needed.

Pass the tomatoes through a mill and add them to the meat. Simmer slowly for 1 hour.
The traditional way to enjoy this dish is on thick slices of toasted Tuscan bread, laid out in a serving dish. You then wet these with the gravy or hot broth and the add the 'Scottiglia' on top.

# *Spezzatino*

## Tuscan Beef Stew

This recipe is typically Florentine that doesn't need you to use the 'soffritto' which you will discover as we go through the recipe. It is a delicious dish and very versatile. It can be enjoyed as a main course or as a pasta sauce, on 'crostini' or served with polenta. Boiled or oven roasted rosemary potatoes are also a wonderful side dish and of course, the only 'gravy' you will need are the juices from the 'spezzatino'. There are lots of exciting things you can do with this recipe.... lets get to work!!

Serves 4 - 6

- 1 kg. Muscle Veal is best – Take the cut of meat from the hind leg that is rich in tendons that cook and melt & make the 'spezzatino' soft & tender. If you use a cut of meat that is very lean your 'spezzatino' will be tough & chewy.
- 3 cloves garlic
- 6 tablespoons of olive oil
- 1 glass of red wine - optional
- 2 tablespoons of flour
- 1 kg chopped tomatoes
- salt & pepper

In a saucepan heat the oil & crushed garlic then add the meat cut into cubes of about 3 cms and brown for about 20 mins. Pay attention that during this stage of the process the garlic doesn't burn because it will give the meat a bitter taste. At this point if you wish you can add the glass of red wine.
Salt & pepper to taste and then add the sifted flour. The flour is added to allow the sauce to 'stick' to the meat.
Stir well and after about 3 mins add the chopped tomatoes, lower the flame and allow to cook, covered for about 1.5 hours. Like all stews, allow the meat to cool a little before serving, it is much nicer not steaming hot.
In Tuscany this stew is typically made with potatoes. When the meat is three quarters done add about ½ kilo of peeled and diced potatoes. If it seems too dry you can add some broth.

# *Stracotto alla fiorentina*

## Florentine pot roast

Serves 6

- Beef (rump or rolled topside): 1,2 Kg
- Ripe or canned plum tomatoes: 450 g
- l cup red wine
- 1 onion
- 2 stalks celery
- 2 medium sized carrots
- 2 garlic cloves
- olive oil
- salt and pepper

Flavour the meat with salt, pepper and garlic, secure with string, like a salami. Place half a cup of oil, the finely chopped onion, carrot and celery in a casserole dish. Add the meat and sauté well on all sides over a high heat. Turn continually for about half an hour, add the red wine and, when this has evaporated completely, add the tomatoes.
Cover the casserole dish and let simmer over a low heat for about two and a half hours, turning the meat often and adding a little water, if necessary.
When the meat is "stracotto" (very well-cooked), remove from the casserole dish and keep hot, remove all the fat you can (keep this for making sauces), then strain the rest of the sauce.
After a few minutes, heat once again, untie the meat and cut into slices; arrange on a serving dish and pour the hot sauce over the top.

# *Arrosto di vitello ripieno*

## Oven baked of beef or veal

Serves 5

- 500 gr block piece of beef or veal
- 2 slices of tuscan proscuitto
- 2 slices of mortadella
- 2 eggs
- 1 ball of boiled spinach (or see recipe 'Florentine Spinach')
- 20gr butter
- salt & pepper

For this recipe you can use either rump steak or the same cut of veal. If you can get more of a cube, it then needs to be cut in a way that it makes one long flat piece. This piece of meat should be around 3 cms thick when flat.
Pre-heat oven to 180°C. Soften the meat with a meat tenderizer.
First you make an omelette: whisk the eggs, adding a pinch of salt. Cut the spinach and cook in a saucepan with 2 tablespoons of olive oil. The spinach will reduce in size and become more moist. Add the beaten eggs and cook for 5-8 mins covered on a low-medium flame.
Take the meat and lay it flat on a large piece of baking paper. Place over the meat the slices of prosciutto, the spinach omelette and the mortadella slices. Roll the meat making a large salami , then tie together using kitchen string. Wipe over with butter and then make a 'package' around the meat with the baking paper.
This then needs to be baked for 1.5 hours at 180°C.

# *Quaglie alla Fiorentina*

## Florentine quails

Serves 4

- 8 quails
- 8 slices of bacon
- 50 g Butter
- A bunch of parsley, thyme and bay leaves
- White wine
- A little broth
- 8 slices of bread
- Olive oil
- Salt and pepper

Clean the quails well, salt and pepper inside, then cover their breasts with slices of bacon. Hold the legs to the body and secure these and the bacon with a string.
Place in a casserole dish, together with the butter, 3 spoonfuls of olive oil and the bunch of herbs and sauté over a high heat.
When these have browned, pour the wine over the top and allow to evaporate. Continue to cook adding a little broth every now and then.
When the quails are very tender, remove the herbs; untie and serve with their sauce (if there is too much liquid, thicken with a little flour) on toasted bread dipped lightly into the broth on one side only.

# *Vitello tonnato*

## Veal with tuna sauce

Serves 8

**For the sauce:**

- 100 g canned tuna
- 1 Tbs capers
- 5 anchovy fillets
- 1.5 cup mayonnaise
- salt
- white pepper
- lemon juice from ¼ of a lemon

To make the sauce put all the ingredients except the mayonnaise into a food processor. Then mix in the mayonnaise and lemon juice. If the sauce is too thick, add a bit of the veal cooking juices.

**For the veal:**

- 2 x 750g veal
- 3 anchovy fillets
- 1 carrot
- 1 celery stalk
- 1 onion
- 3 garlic cloves
- 1 bay leaf
- 2 parsley stalks
- ½ lemon
- ½ cup dry white wine
- water
- extra anchovies
- capers

In a large saucepan place the veal (which should fit quite snugly), the vegetables, garlic, anchovies, herbs and ½ a lemon. Cover the meat with the boiling water and wine. Simmer gently for about 2 hours until the meat is tender. It is best if the meat is allowed to cool down in its own juices even in the fridge overnight. Slice the veal very thinly and serve, pouring the sauce over and garnishing it with a few capers.

# *Seppie inzimino*

## Cuttle fish and spinach stew

Serves 4

- 800 g cuttle fish/calamari
- 1 kg spinach with the thick part of the stalk removed, sliced thinly
- 400 g chopped, peeled tomatoes
- 1 onion, chopped finely
- 1 carrot, chopped finely
- 1 celery stalk, chopped finely
- 2–3 garlic cloves, chopped finely
- 2 dried chillies, crushed
- 150 ml dry white wine
- extra virgin olive oil
- salt

De-bone the cuttle fish and remove the intestine, ink bag, skin, and beak. Slice the cuttle fish into 1 cm wide strips. Sautè onion, carrot, celery, garlic and chili in 8 tbs of olive oil. Add the cuttle fish and cook for a few minutes. Add the wine and let it evaporate. Add the tomatoes and salt and cook for about 20 minutes. Add the spinach. Cook for another 20 minutes or until the cuttlefish is soft, adding a bit more liquid if necessary. Serve with plenty of bread on the table.

# *Seppie ripiene*

## Stuffed cuttle fish /calamari

- 4 x 200 g cuttlefish/calamari
- 2 eggs
- 4 Tbs breadcrumbs
- 2 Tbs grated parmesan cheese
- 1 Tbs butter, softened
- 2 garlic cloves, chopped finely
- 4 sprigs of parsley, chopped finely
- 1 pinch of salt
- 1 pinch of ground black pepper
- 200 ml dry white wine
- 300 g peeled chopped tomatoes
- 200 ml vegetable or fish broth
- 8 Tbs extra virgin olive oil
- salt and ground black pepper

De-bone the cuttlefish/calamari and remove the intestine, ink bag, skin, and beak. Cut the thin end of the tentacles and chop them. Mix tentacles, bread crumbs, parmesan, butter, eggs, salt and pepper. Stuff the cuttlefish with the mixture then close them with toothpicks. In a pan sautè the garlic and cuttlefish. Add the wine, let it evaporate then add the tomatoes and the broth. Cook for around ½ an hour. Add more broth if necessary. When the cuttlefish/calamari are soft, add the parsley and cook for another couple of minutes. Add salt if necessary.

**Alternative:** *These can also be prepared in the oven without the tomatoes or the broth.*
*Place the calamari on a baking pan that is covered with baking paper. Drizzle the remaining olive oil over the pieces of calamari.*

# *Baccalà con i porri*

## Salted cod with leeks

Serves 6

- 1 kg soaked salted cod
- 600 g leeks
- 300 g peeled chopped tomatoes
- 100 ml water
- 8 Tbs olive oil
- 1–2 dry cayenne chili peppers, crumbed
- a pinch of salt
- a pinch of ground black pepper

Clean and wash the leeks well, discard the tough, deep green part and slice them quite thinly. Sautè the oil with the chillies in a pan and add the leeks, cooking them gently until soft. Then add the tomatoes, water and salt and cook for a further 10 minutes. In the meantime, skin and bone the cod then cut it into about 5 cm pieces and add it to the pan. Cook for a further 15 minutes.

# *Branzino all' Isolana*

## Baked sea bass with mixed vegetables

Serves 4

- 2 x 500 g sea bass, scaled and gutted
- 4 potatoes, diced
- 2 zucchini, diced
- 4 tomatoes, diced
- 8 black olives, pitted and halved
- 2 garlic cloves, crushed
- 4 artichoke hearts, sliced
- oregano
- ground black pepper
- olive oil
- salt

Put the potatoes, tomatoes and zucchini in a baking dish. Add the oregano, olives, garlic, salt and pepper and put in a 185° C oven for about 20 minutes. Then add the artichokes and fish and put back in the oven for another 25 minutes. Fillet the fish and serve immediately with the vegetables.

**Alternative:** *This dish is also very nice prepared wth just cherry tomatoes and potatoes. You will need to peel and thinly slice the potatoes and make a 'bed' on the bottom of the baking dish, add some of the cherry tomatoes (chopped in half), a generous dash of olive oil, some rosemary and sage (optional), salt and pepper and then lay the fish on top (be sure to pat the fish dry if you have washed it), covering with the remaining cherry tomatoes. Like the recipe above you can add olives and also flaked almonds for a different touch. Bake in 185°C preheated oven for around 25-30 minutes.*

# *Contorni*

## Side Dishes

# *Flan di verdure*

## Multi colour vegetable flan

Serves 6

*You can use whichever vegetables you like for this flan, your imagination is your only limitation.*

- 800 g leek, carrot, zucchini, broccoli or cauliflower...
- ½ L liquid cream
- 4 whole eggs
- 4 egg whites
- grated parmesan
- salt and pepper
- 4 Tbs olive oil

Cut your chosen vegetable/s into small pieces, wash and then cook in a saucepan with the olive oil over on a medium flame for about 25 minutes. Let cool, then place in a bowl adding all of the remaining ingredients. With a hand mixer (not beaters), blend all ingredients together.
Take small moulds, similar to those you would use for creme caramel, then cover all of the inside with a light coating of melted butter. Fill the moulds to about ¾ with the mixture.
Place the moulds in a baking dish filled to about ¾ with water. This creates a bain-marie. Place carefully in the oven to cook at 160°C for 40 mins.
For the multi-colour flan you need to follow the same directions, but cook different types of vegetables separately then proceed to make the cream/vegetable mixture as above. When you reach the point of filling the moulds, just alternate the different colours as you like.

## *Melanzane alla parmigiana*

### Eggplant parmesan

Serves 6

- 2 large eggplants
- 1 L of sunflower oil
- 1 Tbs of flour
- 3 cups of tomato sauce with basil
- 1 mozzarella ball (or enough mozzarella in sheets)
- 1 cup of grated parmesan

Remove the stem from each eggplant. Cut the eggplant into 1/2 cm slices. Dust each eggplant slice with flour and fry on both sides until golden brown. Drain on paper towel. Line a baking dish with a little of the tomato sauce, arrange a layer of eggplant slices and cover with a layer of mozzarella cheese, more tomato sauce and sprinkling of grated parmesan cheese. Repeat the layers until all ingredients are used and finish with tomato sauce. Bake in a preheated 180°/350 degree oven for 30 minutes Garnish with chopped fresh basil and serve.

## *Piselli alla Fiorentina*

### Florentine-style peas

Serves 4

- 500 g peas
- 2 garlic cloves
- a couple of sprigs of parsley
- 100 g  diced pancetta
- 4 Tbs extra virgin olive oil
- olive oil
- salt and pepper

Put the peas, garlic and parsley in a pot and cover with cold water. Salt lightly and cook on a moderate flame for around 30 minutes. A minute before removing from the flame, add the pancetta and add salt and pepper to taste.

# *Fagioli all'olio*

## Beans with oil

Serves 4-6

- 400 g dry cannellini beans
- 2 L cold water
- 2 garlic cloves
- 2 Tbs extra virgin olive oil
- 1 sprig of sage
- 1 tsp salt
- a few peppercorns

Wash the cannellini beans and put them in a pot. Add the water, garlic, oil, sage, salt and pepper. Cover with a lid and place over a really low flame. The water must simmer very gently and not boil. The beans will take about 2 - 3 hours to cook. Let them cool in the cooking juices. Before serving, heat them until warm, taste for salt and black pepper and drizzle with good extra virgin olive oil.

# *Ceci lessi*

## Boiled chickpeas

Serves 4 - 6

- 400 g dry chickpeas
- 2 garlic cloves
- 2 Tbs extra virgin olive oil
- 1 sprig of rosemary
- 1 tsp salt
- a few peppercorns

Soak the chickpeas overnight and put them in a pot with 2 litres of water. Add the water, garlic, oil, rosemary, salt and pepper. Cover with a lid and place over a low flame. The water must simmer gently and not boil. The chickpeas will take around 2 hours to cook. Let them cool in the cooking juices. Before serving, heat them up until warm, taste for salt and black pepper and drizzle with good extra virgin olive oil.

# *Fagiolini alla Fiorentina*

## Florentine-style green beans

Serves 4

- 800 g green beans, with the tips trimmed off
- 400 g peeled chopped tomatoes
- ½ red onion, chopped finely
- 2 garlic cloves, chopped finely
- 1 carrot, chopped finely
- 100 ml olive oil
- 2 pinches of salt
- 1 pinch of ground black pepper

Sautè the onion and carrot in the oil. Add the green beans and cook for a few minutes. Add the tomatoes, salt and pepper and simmer for about 30 minutes until the green beans are soft.

# *Sedani ripieni*

## Stuffed celery

Serves 4

- 8 large celery stalks, cleaned of their strings
- 150 g chicken livers, with the bitter green part removed, chopped finely
- 300 g veal mince
- 1 small onion, chopped finely
- 1 carrot, chopped finely
- 50 g butter
- 1 egg
- 70 g grated parmesan cheese
- 2 pinches of salt
- 1 pinch of ground black pepper
- flour
- 200 g peeled chopped tomatoes
- 100 ml water

Blanch the celery sticks in boiling salted water for a couple of minutes. Let them cool and cut them into 8 cm long pieces. Sautè the onion and carrot in the butter. When the onion is soft, add the chicken livers and the mince. Put the mixture in a bowl, let it cool slightly then add the egg, parmesan, salt and pepper and mix well. Spoon the mixture onto half of the celery stalks, cover these with the remaining celery stalks and tie with kitchen string. Flour them and brown them in the olive oil with the crushed garlic. Add the tomatoes and water. Simmer gently until the celery is soft and has soaked up the juices. Taste for salt and pepper, adjust as necessary and serve.

........................................................................................................

........................................................................................................

# *Spinaci rifatti con l'aglio*

## Spinach with garlic

Serves 4

- 800 g spinach with the thick part of the stalk removed
- 2 garlic cloves, crushed
- 8 Tbs extra virgin olive oil
- a pinch of salt

Wash the spinach twice and cook it using just the water left on the leaves from the rinsing. This should take about 10 minutes though some people prefer the spinach more 'al dente' others more well cooked, so we will let you be the judge. After it has almost cooked to your liking, remove from the pan and squeeze it well. Chop the leaves roughly. Sautè the garlic in the olive oil and add the spinach and the salt. Cook for a few minutes to flavour it and serve.

........................................................................................................

........................................................................................................

........................................................................................................

# *Cavolo strascicato*

## Braised cauliflower

Serves 4

- 1 cauliflower, divided into flowerettes, stalk chopped
- 300 g peeled chopped tomatoes
- 2 garlic cloves, crushed
- 2 pork sausages, skinned and chopped
- 100 g black olives, pitted
- 100 ml white vinegar
- 100 ml olive oil
- 1 Tbs rock salt
- 1 tsp salt
- a pinch of pepper

Bring a pot with 4 litres of water and the vinegar to the boil. Then add the rock salt and blanch the cauliflower in it for 3 minutes from the moment the water comes back to the boil again. Drain it and set aside. Sautè the garlic and the sausages with the olive oil. Add the cauliflower, salt and pepper. After a few minutes, add the tomatoes and simmer for about 20 minutes. Add the olives 5 minutes before turning off the heat.

# *Patate salvia e rosmarino*

## Roasted potatoes with sage and rosemary

Serves 4 - 6

- 1 kg potatoes, peeled and cut into cubes
- 3-4 Tbs extra virgin olive oil
- 4 garlic cloves, unpeeled and lightly crushed
- the leaves of 4 sprigs of fresh rosemary, chopped finely
- 2 sage leaves, chopped finely
- a good pinch of salt
- a pinch of black pepper

Preheat oven to 180°C. Rub the potato cubes completely dry. Put them in a baking dish with the oil and garlic. Toss them and place them in the oven. Bake for about 45 minutes until potatoes are golden and cooked through. Mix together the rosemary, sage, salt and pepper. Stir the herb mix through the potatoes a couple minutes before ending the roasting process. Serve.

## *Mamme ripiene*

### Stuffed artichokes

Serves 4

- 4 'Mamme' artichokes
- 8 slices of pancetta ham
- 2 garlic cloves
- 1 bunch of parsley
- 8 Tbs olive oil
- salt and pepper
- ½ cup water
- 1 lemon

Clean the artichokes by pulling off the harder outside leaves, cut off about 2 cms at the top and then cut off (and save!) the stem so that the artichoke stands upright on its end. Chop finely the pancetta, garlic, parsley, lemon rind and the stem of the artichoke and mix together in a bowl. This makes the 'ripieno', which means 'stuffing'. Salt and pepper as required.
Pull apart slightly the leaves of the artichoke to create an opening in the centre and then push in the stuffing.
Place the olive oil in a saucepan or non stick fry pan, then on top place the stuffed artichokes, with the leaves facing upwards, so that they are sitting on their base, add the water, cover and let cook over a low flame for an hour.

# *Melanzane Ripiene*

## Stuffed eggplants

Serves 4

- 2 ripe eggplant
- 4 ripe roma tomatoes
- 2 teaspoon of capers
- 3 anchovy fillets
- herbs: basil, parsley, oregano, thyme, tarragon
- salt and pepper
- 2 slices bread
- vinegar

Preheat oven to 150°C. Wash and vertically cut the eggplant. With a teaspoon remove the insides of the eggplant to make a hole. Place eggplant flesh in a bowl.

In another bowl mix 4 teaspoons of vinegar with some cold water and place the bread into this liquid. In another bowl mix together the chopped tomatoes and the other ingredients with 4 tablespoons of olive oil. Squeeze the bread and mix with the mixture of tomato adding salt and pepper. Use this mixture to stuff the eggplant.

Take a baking dish and line with baking paper. Place the eggplant, sprinkle with more herbs and some olive oil and cook for 1 hour or until tender.

# *Polpettine di rape e ricotta al pomodoro fresco*

## Spinach and ricotta balls with fresh tomato sauce

**For the tomato and basil sauce recipe: refer to page 78.**

Serves 4

- 400 g cooked spinach
- 200 g ricotta
- 2 eggs
- grated parmesan cheese

- a garlic clove
- parsley
- breadcrumbs
- handmade breadcrumbs
- olive oil
- salt and peppercorns

Finely chop the garlic and parsley together. Place a handful of the roughly broken up breadcrumbs to soak in either water of milk. Chop the spinach and mix with the ricotta, the eggs and a couple of teaspoons of parmesan, salt and pepper. Squeeze out the bread and mix this in also.
Mix all of the ingredients well and then form small balls with your hands, roughly the size of an egg. They can be round or oval in shape. Rolls the balls in the fine breadcrumbs and fry them in a sauce pan with some the preheated olive oil. Finish the cooking with some tomato and basil sauce.

## *Cipolle ripiene con pecorino*

### Onion stuffed with pecorino

Serves 6

- 6 onions (white or red)
- 12 cloves
- 2 egg yolks
- 200 grated pecorino cheese (a harder one is preferred)
- breadcrumbs
- salt and pepper

Preheat the oven to 180°C. Clean the onions and grate them halfway. Stick a clove inside each onion and place in a saucepan with a little water, salt and oil then cover and let cook on a slow flame.
Once cooked you will need to empty the onions, leaving only about 3 layers internally. Chop the onion you have removed then mix with the egg yolks, and cheese then place the mixture back into the onion centre. Sprinkle with the breadcrumbs then place into the oven to allow them to slightly brown on top.

# *Carciofi trifolati*

## Artichokes

Serves 6

- 12 artichokes
- 1 lemon
- 2 cloves of garlic
- 6 Tbs of olive oil
- parsley
- salt and pepper
- 1 cup of hot water

In a bowl squeeze the lemon juice into cold water.
Clean the artichokes (cut half of the stalk off, about 2-3 cms from the tips and remove the external leaves, the hard ones). Immediately brush with the lemon to prevent the artichokes from turning black when exposed to the air. Cut the artichokes in half and then cut in thin slices, place them in a bowl. Take a saucepan and add the olive oil, the pressed cloves of garlic and parsley. When the oil is hot remove the artichokes from the water and cook for 5 minutes on a hot flame, stirring continually. Lower the flame, add salt and pepper, cover and cook for about 30 minutes. Pay attention as if the steam is not sufficient to cook the artichokes (this will depend on the quality and freshness of the artichokes and the strength of the gas), add a little hot water, a little at a time. You will know when they are cooked when they are soft but not falling apart.

# *Cipolline in agrodolce all'aceto balsamico*

## Sweet and sour onions

Serves 8
- 1 kg 'borrettane' onions - these are the small flat variety
- 3 tablespoons of sugar
- 8 tablespoons of extra virgin olive oil
- 300 ml balsamic vinegar
- 1 bay leaf

Peel, wash and dry the onions. Add the bay leaf to the oil, then add the whole onions making sure to not move them too much allowing them to take a lovely golden colour.
After they are golden add the sugar and allow to dissolve and caramelize.
After this add the balsamic vinegar and let cook for another 20 mins until they are soft.
If necessary during the cooking process you can add a little water or vegetable broth.

# *Dolci*

## Dessert

# *Castagnaccio*

## Tuscan Chestnut flat cake

- 400 gr sweet chestnut flour
- 100 gr raisins
- 50 gr pine nuts
- 50 gr crushed walnuts
- fresh sprig rosemary
- 2 spoons of sugar ( dessert spoon size not teaspoon)
- salt
- olive oil
- ½ litre of cold water

Put the raisins in some water to soak.
Sift the flour and place in a large bowl, add the sugar, a pinch of salt then pour in half a litre of cold water and stir very well. Blend so there are no lumps.
Add 2 spoons of olive oil and the raisins, stir again then pour into a rectangle baking dish that has been greased with olive oil. The mixture should be 1 finger in height.
Cover the surface of the mixture with pine nuts, the walnuts that have been crushed and a little of the rosemary leaves form the sprig.

Place in a preheated 200 ° C oven after pouring a little bit of olive oil on top. Cook for 30 minutes. The surface should be golden and a little crunchy.

# *Tiramisù*

## Traditional Italian soft cake to be served with the spoon

"Tiramisù" actually translates to "Pick Me Up", due to the sugar and caffeine in the recipe.

Serves 6

- 3 large eggs, separated
- 3 Tbs fine sugar
- 250 g mascarpone cheese
- 2 Tbs of a coffee liqueur or marsala
- 500 ml coffee
- 200 g pavesini or lady finger cookies
- cocoa powder

With an electric mixer, beat the egg yokes and sugar until the mixture is thick and pale. Add the marscarpone and keep whisking. Mix in the coffee liqueur and set aside. In a large bowl, whisk the egg whites and a pinch of salt until firm. Using a spatula, gently fold them into the marscapone mixture. Place the cold coffee in a shallow bowl. Dip the biscuits in the coffee then place them in the serving dish in a single layer. Pour the mascarpone mixture on top of the layer of biscuits. Place another layer of coffee-soaked biscuits on top and repeat the process until all biscuits have been used. The last layer of the tiramisù is a layer of the marscapone mixture. Cover the dish with cling film and chill for a few hours. Before serving, dust the tiramisù with cocoa powder or freshly grated chocolate. The end result is a soft, creamy dessert to be eaten with a spoon.

# *Pannacotta*

## Cooked cream

- 1 L of liquid cream
- 200 g of fine white sugar
- 1 tsp of vanilla essence
- 4 small sheets of gelatin

Slightly heat the cream in a saucepan, add the sugar and vanilla and stir well. Place the sheets of gelatin in a cup of cold water. Leave for 3 minutes and this will soften the gelatin. After the 3 minutes squeeze out the water and place the sheets into the cream mixture, stirring continuously to mix well on a medium flame until it almost boils. Place the mixture into the mould and place into the fridge for 3 hours. When you are ready to serve, turn the mould upside down onto the plate or serving dish. This can be served with cream, chocolate or a sauce made with fresh fruit.

# *Bavarese alla Frutta*

## Fruity Bavarian Cream

Serves 6

- 250 gr of fruit
- 250 ml of fresh liquid cream
- 100 gr castor sugar
- 10 gr gelatin

Place the gelatin in cold water. In a saucepan combine the fruit and sugar and on a low heat allow the sugar to dissolve in with the fruit. Purée the fruit mixture. While still warm add the softened gelatin sheets and allow to melt. Let to sit in the fridge until the mixture is semi-solid, like a thick yoghurt. Whip the cream and when thickened fold into the fruit purée mixture. Place in the moulds or single serves bowls, however you choose to serve the dessert. Let chill in the fridge for 3 hours. Serve decorated with fresh fruit

# *Salsa di cioccolato*

## Chocolate sauce

- 200 g of dark chocolate
- 15 g butter
- 1 glass of milk

Put the chocolate and butter in a metal mixing bowl over another saucepan of boiling water. Melt these ingredients together until you have a smooth liquid consistency. Add the glass of milk slowly, constantly stirring. Let cool slightly and then pour over a dessert such as pannacotta.

# *Salsa di frutta*

## Fruit sauce

- Fruit of your choice
- 2 Tbs sugar

Prepare the fruit, cutting off any stalks or seeds, place into the pan with the sugar and cook over a medium flame for 10 minutes, stirring constantly. Once this mixture is soft enough you then need to pass this through a sieve of some sort to form a liquid and remove any pips or seeds. If you wish you can also add half a glass of liqueur - Grand Marnier, Brandy or Cointreau are all good. If you do add the alcohol, cook again in the pan for 5 minutes to take off the strong alcohol taste. It's ready!

# *Crostata di ricotta e marmellata di mirtilli*

## Ricotta and blueberry jam tart

Serves 8-12

**For the pastry: see a short crust recipe on page 151.**

- 2 quantities short crust pastry
- 500 g cow's milk ricotta
- 250 g blueberry jam
- 60 g icing sugar
- 2 pinches cinnamon powder
- 1 egg to seal the tart

Mix the ricotta, icing sugar and cinnamon. Roll the pastry to a thickness of about 3 mm and cut out 2 disks, one bigger than the other. Put the smaller one into the fridge. Line a 26 cm diameter tart tin with the bigger disk. Chill or freeze the pastry base for at least 30 minutes prior to baking. It can be baked whilst frozen. Once chilled, line the pastry with foil and cover with dried beans or rice. Bake at 200° C for 10 minutes, then remove the foil and beans/rice before baking the pastry base for a further 5 minutes. Spread the jam onto the base then add the ricotta. Brush the edges with a beaten egg then put the lid on and secure it. Cook in a 200 °C oven for about 12 minutes until the pastry is golden. Let it cool, remove from the mould and serve with a dusting of icing sugar.

# *Pesche caramellate con zabaione al vin santo*

## Caramelised peaches with vin santo sabayon

Serves 4

**For the sabayon:**

- 4 egg yolks
- 150 g sugar
- 4 - 5 half egg shells of sweet vin santo wine

Whisk the egg yolks and sugar until pale and creamy. As you whisk slowly add the vin santo. Bring some water to simmering point in a pot and put the bowl with the sabayon over the pot, ensuring that the water doesn't come into contact with the base of the bowl. Keep whisking continuously until the sabayon starts to thicken up. Then partially immerse the bowl in cold water and keep whisking for 5 minutes until the sabayon has cooled down.

**For the peaches:**

- 2 tsp honey
- 2 peaches, peeled and sliced into wedges
- 1 vanilla pod, halved
- 1 Tbs unsalted butter

Heat the honey in a pan on a high flame. Add the peaches and toss them for a minute. Lower the flame and add the butter and the vanilla pod. Cook for another couple of minutes. Place the peaches into 4 individual bowls and cover with the room temperature sabayon.

# *Gelato al vin santo*

## Vin santo ice cream

Serves 4

- 4 egg yolks
- 150 g fine sugar
- 150 ml vin santo wine
- 400 ml full cream milk
- 100 ml milk cream

Whisk the egg yolks with the sugar until pale yellow and creamy, add the vin santo and mix it through. Heat up cream and milk then add to the egg yolks and transfer to a bain marie. Cook for a few minutes, stirring constantly until the cream coats the back of a spoon. Let it cool and place into a gelato machine. When the gelato reaches a thick creamy consistency put it into the freezer for 20 minutes and serve.

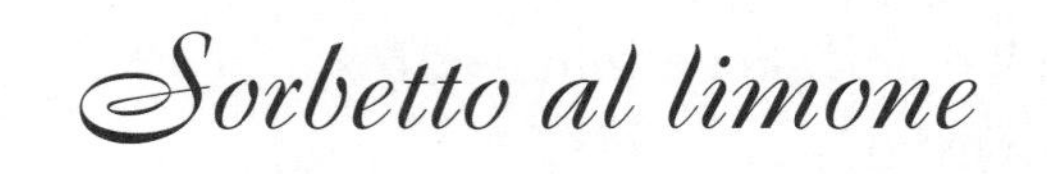


## Lemon sorbet

Serves 4

- 200 g sugar
- 3 unwaxed juicy lemons
- 500 ml water
- 50 ml grappa or vodka

Prepare a syrup in a saucepan with the water, sugar and the zest of one of the lemons. Let it cool and discard the zest. Add the grappa and juice of the 3 lemons. Put in an icecream machine until the mixture reaches the right consistency (for about 15-20 minutes). Put in the freezer for 10 minutes and serve.

# *Spuma al cioccolato*

## Chocolate mousse

Serves 4

- 250 g dark chocolate
- 50 g butter
- 1 vanilla bean, split and seeded
- 50 g sugar
- 4 egg yolks
- 4 egg whites
- a pinch of salt
- a Tbs icing sugar

Break the chocolate and put it in a bowl with the butter and the vanilla bean and seeds. Melt over a bain marie and set aside. Whisk the egg yolks and sugar until pale and creamy. Fold into the chocolate, take out the vanilla bean. Whisk the egg whites with a pinch of salt. When they start to get bubbly, add the icing sugar and keep whisking until stiff peaks form. Delicately fold the egg white into the chocolate and egg yolk mixture. Pour into cups and put in the fridge for a few hours. Serve, garnishing with untreated orange zest (blanched in hot water for a couple of minutes).

# *Bomboloni*

## Donuts

Serves 6 - 8

- 250 g flour
- 4 g salt
- 50 g sugar
- 50 g butter
- 2 eggs
- 100 ml water
- 12 g fresh yeast

Dissolve the yeast in 50 ml of water and mix in a teaspoon of flour. Set aside for 15 minutes. Then mix the flour, salt, sugar, butter, eggs, yeast and the rest of the water and work it with your hands until you obtain a smooth dough. Cover and let it rise in a warm place for half an hour. Work the dough briefly and roll it to a thickness of 1 cm. Cut it into circles of about 6 cm diameter. Place the disks on a floured surface in a warm place. Lightly grease the sides exposed to the air to prevent them from drying out. Let them rise until they double in volume which should take about an hour. Fry them in plenty of oil (165 °C) until golden on both sides. Drain them and place them on kitchen paper. Roll them in the sugar and serve hot.

# *Frittelle di riso*

## Sweet rice dumplings

Serves 6

- 150 g rice
- 750 ml milk
- 1 Tbs sugar
- 40 g butter
- a pinch of salt
- the zest of one non-waxed lemon

- 75 g flour
- 3 eggs, separated
- 50 g sultanas, soaked in 100 ml of vin santo
- peanut oil for frying

Boil the milk with the sugar, salt, zest and butter. Add the rice and cook on a low heat until the rice has absorbed all the liquid. Add the flour, baking flour, egg yolks and sultanas with the vin santo to the warm milk. Let the mixture rest for a couple of hours or more. Whisk the egg whites until stiff peaks form and fold them into the rice mixture. Fry spoonfuls of the mixture in the hot oil until golden. Strain them and drain them on kitchen paper. Roll them in sugar and serve.

## Biscotti di Prato

### Prato-style almond biscuits

Serves 6

- 500 g flour
- 250 g sugar
- 150 g melted, unsalted butter
- 200 g sweet almonds, unpeeled
- 2 eggs plus 1 for brushing
- 3 egg yolks
- 1 sachet baking powder
- the rind of 1 lemon or orange, grated
- a pinch of salt

Arrange the flour like a mountain, form a well in the middle then add sugar, eggs, egg yolks, lemon rind, baking powder and salt. Start working the mixture with your hands. When the mixture is still crumbly, add the butter and keep working until you obtain quite a soft dough. Add the almonds and work it again. Roll the dough into logs that are the length of the baking tray and of a 3–4 cm diameter. Place them on the baking tray lined with baking paper and place in a 180 °C oven for 15 minutes. Then cut the logs on an angle, to form the biscuits and return to oven for a further 5 minutes.

# *Pere cotte nel vino rosso con crema e salsa di vino*

## Pears cooked in red wine and served with vanilla custard and reduced red wine syrup

Serves 4

**For the pears and syrup:**

- 4 williams pears
- 1.5 L red wine (un-oaked)
- 1 tsp cloves
- 2 cinnamon sticks
- 300g sugar

Peel the pears with care and leave the stem on top. You can either leave them whole or cut in half and eliminate the seeds. In a large saucepan add the wine, sugar, cinnamon, and the cloves. Stir and then add the pears so they are completely covered.

Cook over a gentle flame for approximately 20 minutes until they are soft but still quite firm.

The time depends on how mature the pears are and the size. Stir occasionally if they are not completely covered.

Turn off the heat and let them sit in the wine for approximately 20 minutes.

Remove the pears with a large slotted spoon and set aside carefully. Strain the wine to remove the cloves and then boil until the sauce reduces to approximately one third or the desired consistency.

**For the custard:**

- 375 ml whole milk
- 3 egg yolks
- 50 g sugar
- 10 g flour
- 1 vanilla bean, split
- the peel of half a lemon

Mix the flour, egg yolks, sugar and a bit of the milk together in a bowl. In a saucepan (preferably copper) heat the milk with the lemon peel and vanilla until it reaches near boiling point. Slowly add the milk to the egg mixture, stirring constantly, and put back into the saucepan over a low heat, stirring constantly until the sauce thickens.
Serve the pears with the cream and a little of the wine sauce.

## *Latte alla portoghese*

### Crème caramel

Serves 4

- 700 g milk
- 300 g cream
- 300 g cane sugar
- 8 eggs
- peel of 2 oranges

In a saucepan, add the milk and cream. On a slow heat, bring to the boil and then remove from the heat. In a bowl, mix the sugar and the eggs together, then slowly start to add in the milk/cream mix. Using a cake ring mould, cover the base with the peel of 2 oranges and cover with cane sugar. Then add the liquid mixture and place the ring into a baking tray that is half filled with water so as to create a bain-marie.
Bake in a 150°C oven for 1 hour.

# *Torta mantovana*

## Mantovana tea cake

Serves 8

- 1 whole egg
- 4 egg yolks
- 150 g sugar
- 180 g white flour
- 150 g butter
- peel of 1 lemon
- 80 g pine nuts or shaved almonds
- icing sugar

In a bowl, beat the egg, then add 150 g sugar and 50 g icing sugar. Mix well. Very slowly incorporate the melted butter, making sure to mix continuously, then add the flour and lemon peel. After mixing well, pour into a baking tin of approximately 25 cm diameter which has been greased and lined with baking paper. Cover the mixture with the almonds or pinenuts. Bake in a 180°C oven for approximately 45 minutes.
Serve dusted with icing sugar.

# *Cioccolatissimo*

## Chocolate, chocolate, chocolate cake!

Serves 4

- 200 g bitter chocolate
- 200 g butter
- 4 egg whites beaten to stiff peaks
- 50 g flour
- 150 g sugar

Melt the chocolate and butter in a double saucepan. Mix the sugar, egg yolks and the flour in a bowl, then add the chocolate/butter mixture. Mix well. Beat the egg whites until they form stiff peaks and fold into the mixture. Bake for 35 minutes in an oven at temperature 150°C.

# *Schiacciata con l'uva*

## Flat peasant cake with grapes and red wine

Serves 6

- 1 bunch of red grapes picked from the wine
- 600 g flour
- 1 cube or sachet of yeast
- 2 glasses warm water
- 5 Tbs sugar
- half glass of red wine
- olive oil

In a bowl, place the yeast with a teaspoon of sugar, a pinch of salt and 2 tablespoons of olive oil. Mix together and wait for 3 minutes. Add sifted flour, mix together to form a ball of dough. This doesn't need to be kneaded too much. Cut a cross on the top of the dough ball and place in a warm place for 2 hours. You can also use a pre-heated oven, which has been turned off to create a warm place. Remove the grapes from the stalk, wash and place in a bowl. For half of the grapes, leave as is, the other half, mix with the sugar and red wine and leave to marinate for 2 hours while the dough is rising. Take a cookie tray, and cover with grease-proof oven paper. Take half the dough and roll out with a rolling pin until it is about 1.5 cms thick. Place 1/2 of the grapes (without the wine) evenly onto the dough, pressing slightly into the mixture. Take the other half of the dough, rolling this in the same way and then cover the first layer, placing the marinated grapes on top.
Bake in a preheated 150°C oven for about 1 hour.

# *Crostata autunnale*

## Autumn tart

Serves 4

**For the pastry: see Short Crust recipe on page 151.**

**For the filling:**

- 2 Williams pears
- 2 cooking apples
- 2 oranges
- 3 tbs of sultanas/raisins
- 20 almond biscuits
- 2 dessert spoons of sugar
- cinnamon
- shaved almonds

Squeeze the oranges. Cut the fruit into small pieces and then place in a mixing bowl with the raisins to marinate with the juice from the oranges. Remove the short crust from the refrigerator and roll out on oven proof paper. Press into the tart mould. Take the biscuits and break into crumbs between your fingers onto the pastry forming a uneven layer. Place the marinated fruit without the juice onto the pastry and biscuit followed by the squeezed raisins and lastly the shaved almonds. Powder the tart with sugar and a little of the cinnamon then place in a hot oven and cook for 40 minutes at 160°C. To be served with vanilla cream or icecream.

# *Crema di vaniglia*

## Vanilla cream

- 6 eggs
- 100 g sugar
- 1/2 L fresh cream
- 1 sachet of powdered vanilla

Heat the cream with the vanilla on a medium flame. In a bowl lightly beat the egg yolks and the sugar. When the cream is almost boiling add the

sugar and egg mixture, and reduce the heat to a low flame. Keep mixing continuously until the creamy mixture reaches 95°C. Allow to cool slightly before using as a base for all types of desserts. Can be used also in the decoration of various tarts and cakes.

## *Pasta frolla*

### Shortcrust pastry

This is the base for dried fruit tarts, jam tarts, cream tarts and biscuits.

- 250 g flour
- 125 g sugar
- 125 g butter
- 2 eggs
- 1 pinch of salt

Unite the flour with the sugar and create a small mountain of flour with a dip in the center. Cut the butter into small pieces and place it in the center, along with the egg and the salt. Mix quickly, blending all the ingredients, and form a ball. Cover with cling wrap and place in fridge for 1 hour.

The trick to this pastry is that it should not be worked too much with the hands otherwise it will not stay together, it will break! To blend the ingredients it is advisable to use a spatula as the warm hands interfere with the end result and the pastry will become hard. Once you have worked the pastry it must rest in the fridge for 1 hour.

# *Frolla alle mandorle*

## Almond shortcrust

- 250 g flour
- 125 g sugar
- 100 g butter
- 30 g almonds finely chopped
- 2 eggs
- 1 pinch of salt

This pastry is perfect for biscuits and cream filled tarts topped with fresh strawberries!
Use the same procedure as the Pasta Frolla recipe, but incorporate the almonds with the sugar and the flour.

# *Frolla al cioccolato*

## Chocolate shortcrust

- 200 g flour
- 50 g bitter cocoa powder
- 125 g sugar
- 125 g butter
- ½ cup cold water
- 1 egg

Use the same procedure as for the Pasta Frolla, but incorporate the cocoa with the flour and the sugar.

# *Semifreddo ai mirtilli e cioccolato bianco*

## Blueberry semifreddo with white chocolate sauce

Serves 6

- 150 g blueberries
- 70 g sugar
- white rum
- 250 g white chocolate
- 4 egg yolks
- 3 Tbs of milk
- 10 g of gelatin (sheets)
- 4 dl of fresh cream

Place the gelatin in a bowl with cold water. Wash the berries very well and place 2/3 of them in a bowl with the sugar, and bring to boil. Take off the flame and add 1 tablespoon of rum. Add the gelatin, well squeezed, and let melt in the berries mix. Break up the chocolate, and add the milk and let melt using a double saucepan. Take off the heat then add the egg yolks, one at a time and the berry mixture. Let cool, stirring often, and when the mixture starts to thicken up add the whipped cream.
Pour the mixture into smaller aluminium moulds and then place in the fridge for at least 3 hours. Turn out onto your serving plate and decorate with the remaining berries and the remaining chocolate cut into tiny shards.

# *Torta di ricotta*
## Ricotta cake

Serves 6-8
**For pasta frolla: refer to the Short Crust recipe on page 151.**

**For the filling:**
- 250 g ricotta
- 100 g sugar
- 50 g raisins
- 80 g candied cedrò (like a big lemon typical in the south of Italy) - optional
- 3 eggs

Preheat the oven to 170°C. Mix the ricotta cheese with all other ingredients making a creamy mixture that is soft and airy. Roll out the pastry and line a pie dish of 26 cms in diameter. Pour over the ricotta mixture, and bake for around 40 minutes. Serve cold or at least room temperature so that the ricotta can 'set'. Torta di Ricotta is also delicious served with a chocolate sauce.

# *Zuppa inglese*
## Tuscan trifle

Alchermes is a Florentine liqueur that traditionally contained a veritable alchemy of herbs and spices, as well as sugar and a curious ingredient: dye from the kermes insect from which it gets its name and which gave Alchermes its wonderful scarlet colour. Commercially, this liqueur no longer contains insect dye. It is often used to colour pastry and desserts.

Serves 4
- ½ L milk
- 50 g cornstarch
- 4 egg yolks

- 100 g sugar
- 100 g white chocolate
- 100 g fondue chocolate
- 125 g whipping cream
- 2 cup Alchermes
- 300 g Ladyfinger cookies

Whip the egg yolks, sugar and cornstarch together, stirring well.
Heat the milk, then add to the mixture. Place on a medium flame and continue stirring. Boil for 2-3 minutes then remove from the fire.
Divide the batter into two bowls placing the white chocolate in one and the dark chocolate in the other. Chill both mixtures in the refrigerator for one hour. Add 2 tablespoons of whipping cream in both mixtures.

In a glass platter or baking dish, with sides of at least 2 inches in height, line the bottom with a first layer of ladyfingers, dipped in the Alchermes.
Cover ladyfingers in a layer of white chocolate cream.
Continue the layering process alternating between white chocolate cream and dark chocolate cream, ending with the dark chocolate. Garnish with flakes of chocolate.
Chill for at least 6 hours then serve.
Do not serve too cold.

# *Zuccotto*

## Zuccotto icecream trifle

Serves 6

- 200 g Pan di Spagna - a plain cake that is store-bought, as standard ovens do not provide enough ventilation
- 250 g whipped cream
- 300 g fresh ricotta
- 150 g icing sugar
- 80 g dark chocolate pieces
- 80 g mixed glacè fruit
- 30 g bitter cocoa powder
- mixed liqueurs (maraschino, rum, alchermes)

Beat the cream with the icing sugar until it forms stiff peaks, then fold through the ricotta that has been passed through a sieve. Divide the mixture in half and place into two separate mixing bowls. In one bowl add the chocolate pieces and glazed fruit, in the other bowl the cocoa powder. Cut the Pan di Spagna cake in thin slices and wet with the liquor that has been diluted with a few teaspoons of water. With these slices you then need to line a mould in the classical form of a dome. In the centre place the white mixture (with the chocolate pieces and fruit), then make a hole in this mixture where you will pour the chocolate mixture. Push down well, then layer more cake slices which will also have been soaked in the liqueur. Leave in the fridge for 3-4 hours before serving.

This is an 'antique' dessert in Italy, called a 'semifreddo'. It is said to have been invented by the famous Renaissance chef, Buonatalenti, who was a great lover of sweets and above all of gelato. It is he who is the father of the famous flavour of gelato rightly called 'Buontalenti'!

# *Pinolata*

## Pinenut cake

Serves 6

- 250 g sugar
- 250 g room temperature butter
- 4 eggs
- 300 g flour
- pinenuts
- salt
- vanilla
- lemon rind

Cream the butter and sugar together until the consistency is fluffy and light. Next add one egg, stirring in one at a time, but not over-mixing. Then mix in the flour. Place half of the mixture into a cake tin. Next, you will need to make the 'crema pasticciera' as per the recipe. Layer this cream mix on top of the mixture already in the cake tin, before adding the remainder of the cake mixture. Sprinkle with pinenuts, then bake in a 150°C oven for 1 hour.

# *Crema pasticcera*

## Italian pastry cream

Serves 6

- 2 eggs
- 500 ml milk
- 50 g flour
- 150 g sugar
- 1 vanilla bean (optional)

In a saucepan, add the milk, and, if you like, the vanilla bean. Bring the milk to the boil. In a bowl, mix the eggs, flour and sugar together, then slowly add in the heated milk, stirring continuously. Add the entire mixture into the saucepan, over a low heat, and continue stirring until you reach the desired consistency.

# CONVERSION CHART

| WEIGHT EQUIVALENTS | | |
|---|---|---|
| OZ | GRAMS (g) | POUNDS (lb) |
| 1/2 oz | 14 g | 0.03 lb |
| 1 oz | 28 g | 0.06 lb |
| 2 oz | 57 g | 0.13 lb |
| 3 oz | 85 g | 0.19 lb |
| 4 oz | 113 g | 0.25 lb |
| 5 oz | 142 g | 0.31 lb |
| 6 oz | 170 g | 0.38 lb |
| 7 oz | 198 g | 0.44 lb |
| 8 oz | 227 g | 0.50 lb |
| 10 oz | 315 g | 0.63 lb |
| 12 oz | 375 g | 0.75 lb |
| 15 oz | 470 g | |
| 16 oz | 500 g | 0.90 lb |
| 24 oz | 750 g | 1.35 lb |
| 32 oz | 1 kg | 1.8 lb |

| LIQUID MEASURE EQUIVALENTS | | | |
|---|---|---|---|
| CUP | Fl oz | Tbs | ml |
| 1/16 cup | 0.5 oz | 1 Tbs | 15 ml |
| 1/8 cup | 1 oz | 2 Tbs | 30 ml |
| 1/4 cup | 2 oz | 4 Tbs | 59 ml |
| 1/3 cup | 2.7 oz | 5 Tbs + 1 tsp | 79 ml |
| 1/2 cup | 4 oz | 8 Tbs | 118 ml |
| 2/3 cup | 5.3 oz | 10 Tbs + 2 tsp | 158 ml |
| 3/4 cup | 6 oz | 12 Tbs | 177 ml |
| 1 cup | 8 oz | 16 Tbs | 237 ml |

| DRY MEASURE EQUIVALENTS | | |
|---|---|---|
| 1/16 cup | 1 Tbs | 3 tsp |
| 1/8 cup | 2 Tbs | 6 tsp |
| 1/4 cup | 4 Tbs | 12 tsp |
| 1/3 cup | 5 Tbs + 1 tsp | 16 tsp |
| 1/2 cup | 8 Tbs | 24 tsp |
| 2/3 cup | 10 Tbs + 2 tsp | 32 tsp |
| 3/4 cup | 12 Tbs | 36 tsp |
| 1 cup | 16 Tbs | 48 tsp |

| LENGTH MEASURE EQUIVALENTS | |
|---|---|
| 3 mm | 1/8 inch |
| 6 mm | 1/4 inch |
| 1 cm | 1/2 inch |
| 2 cm | 3/4 inch |
| 2.5 cm | 1 inch |
| 6 cm | 2.5 inch |
| 8 cm | 2 inch |
| 20 cm | 8 inch |
| 23 cm | 9 inch |
| 25 cm | 10 inch |
| 30 cm | 12 inch (1 foot) |

| OVEN TEMPERATURES | |
|---|---|
| °C (Celsius) | °F (Fahrenheit) |
| 120 | 250 |
| 150 | 300 |
| 160 | 325 |
| 180-190 | 350-375 |
| 200-210 | 400-425 |
| 220-230 | 450-475 |
| 240-250 | 500-525 |

# Indice delle ricette - Recipe index

## *Antipasti* - Starters

## *Primi piatti* - First Courses

## *Salse e sughi* - Sauces



## *Secondi Piatti* - Mains

## *Contorni* - Side Dishes



## *Dolci* - Dessert

Finito di stampare nel mese di luglio 2012
presso Nova Arti Grafiche, Signa (FI)
per conto di Masso delle Fate Edizioni
Via Cavalcanti, 9/D - 50058 Signa (FI)
massodellefate@novaartigrafiche.it